Fifty-Two Steps Underground:
An Autobiography of a Miner

Ernie Ronn

Center for Upper Peninsula Studies
Northern Michigan University
Marquette

Dedicated to
Negaunee miners, merchants,
and their families.

ISBN# 0-9666248-1-5 paper

Contents

Foreword

This book is about some of the hardy miners who developed the iron ore industry in the Upper Peninsula of Michigan during the first half of the twentieth century. It is told in very descriptive style by Ernie Ronn.

Whereas the book relates to mining and living in the Negaunee, Michigan area, the same story could be easily repeated wherever iron ore and copper mines operated in the Upper Peninsula.

It is the story of hard work, strong ethics, loyalty, humor, and gentleness among many people from more than 14 different nationalities – all of whom regarded themselves as families regardless of their nationality.

The singing of "Silent Night" on Christmas Eve in "finnish" deep in the mines cannot help but bring tears to everyone's eyes.

It vividly describes the miner's homes, their clothing, their food, their entertainment, their health care, their transportation, their religious life, their recreation, their good times and their bad times. The book is a preservation of "How things were" – it is a living history of unbelievable hardship in a continual pursuit of a better life.

It is a story of men who mined iron ore that went to our steel mills and helped make this nation the industrial power it is in the world today.

This book is a must reading for those who cherish the history of the Upper Peninsula.

Ellwood A. Mattson
Retired banker, community leader,
and longtime friend of Ernie Ronn

Introduction

Over the years many have asked me about relatives who worked in underground mines or the way we lived in the "old days." During some of these conversations, many have urged me to "write it down before it's too late." I have asked myself if they know something that I don't. Do they fear my loss of memory, or worse, that I have only limited time to write it down? Should one of my limited education or experience in writing be asked for such a history? Why me?

Since the beginning of mining iron ore on the Marquette Range, many have written and spoken about this industry. Let there be no doubt that I cannot match the excellence of their words, whether they come from pen or by mouth. All have been works of the better educated and more qualified. Yet, if I can provide some information for others who seek to know of underground miners and how they lived, I will do what I can to keep the memories of those good people and their times alive.

This I know: on the historic date of September 19, 1844, little did government surveyor William Burt and his crew realize what their discovery or iron would ultimately mean to our region, state, nation, world, and especially to the economic growth of the Lake Superior District. Even the great California Gold Rush some five years later could not match the contribution of iron to our well being as a nation.

Though much has been recorded of this important discovery, less has been recorded of other necessary developments that gave real value to Mr. Burt's discovery: people of wealth who dared to invest, develop and equip the mine, and men who dared to go underground and actually mine the iron ore and bring it to the surface. Not only did these pioneers prove to be among the best in the world, they passed to us a rich heritage and more importantly, lessons on how people can live in harmony. Although they came from many lands, spoke different languages, and practiced varying customs, beliefs, and religions, they set a standard for living among each other that, in my opinion, has seldom been matched and never improved.

I shall not use fictitious names or alter in any way the words, language, or stores of those miners. In my opinion, this would bring disrespect and dishonor to the most respectable and honorable people anyone could ever hope to meet.

Without question, I consider myself to have been most fortunate to have lived and worked among men of the round-pointed shovel and the miner's pick for most of my life.

Ernie Ronn

Ernie Ronn at the Negaunee Mine. Fall 1999

Historical Perspective

Ernest H. "Ernie" Ronn was "born to be a miner" in 1925. He came into the world in a Cleveland Cliff owned hospital in Ishpeming. A company doctor delivered him and he was taken by his parents Eino and Hilda to a company-owned home on Ann Street in "Swede Town" a location in Negaunee.

His grandfather, Otto Ronn, immigrated from Finland in 1892 and his maternal grandfather, Otto Marttinen arrived a year later from the same country. Both men went to work in the mines. Most of Ernie's family worked and continues to work for Cleveland Cliffs Iron Company. By his calculations, five generations of the Ronn family have labored more than 400 years for CCI.

In June 1943, right out of high school, Ernie got a job in the Negaunee Mine where he joined his father. This was an underground soft-ore mine, with a vertical shaft of only 1,490 feet. Between 1944 and 1946, Ernie was called to active duty in the U.S. Army, serving in Europe. Upon his return to the Upper Peninsula, he was re-employed by CCI.

In the late 1940s the United Steel Workers of America gained representation of the mines' hourly employees. Ernie's long concern for his fellow miners caught the attention of the union leadership. In January 1959 he left the mines and was named staff representative for the district, now known as District 2. During these peak years there were over 10,000 miners in the region. As representative, Ernie dealt with arbitration, grievances, legislative concerns and negotiations. During the 1970s he served as chair of the Federal Mine Safety and Health Advisory Committee. This body, composed of labor and business representatives and safety officials, proposed standards to the Secretary of Interior, Rogers Morton. After a career spanning 44 years in which he worked with and for miners, Ernie retired on May 1, 1987. He was inducted into the Upper Peninsula Labor Hall of Fame a decade later.

If Ernie was "born to be a miner" he is certainly the appropriate person to pen this autobiographical study. He grew up with immigrant miners. Since he was one of them, these Finnish miners talked and confided in him. If an outsider approached them to learn their story, having to use an interpreter, the miners would immediately ask, "Who's that man?" and clam up. Given the labor conditions in the first half of the twentieth century, these miners were apprehensive about talking even to a scholarly interviewer. So it is through Ernie that we get a glimpse of life and labor on a corner of the Marquette Iron Range.

For Ernie interest in the project gradually developed. Over the years he had read scholarly and popular accounts of the life and times on the Marquette Iron Range, but there was something missing. It has been his dream to provide readers with his perspective of the mining experience.

Actual writing goes back to 1979 when CCI engineer and historian, Burt Boyum invited Ernie to write some selections for Boyum's The Mather Mine. Ernie was pleased to do this because over the years friends and acquaintances frequently asked him about life in the mines and individuals who worked there. There were colorful characters who people wanted to know more about that he had encountered and remembered. For a number of years, Ernie would write his ideas on napkins or whatever was available. These scraps were then given to Shirley Mattson and Mary Stone who compiled them into a first draft.

Ernie's autobiography is one of a few which present life and labor on the Marquette Iron Range. It is also significant because it chronicles an important part of regional history. Until the mid-twentieth century, most conventional studies usually dealt with the extraordinary actors on the historical stage. These individuals had the records upon which the histories were based and power and prestige to have these studies published. During the post-World War II era, there was a movement to take a new look at the human experience "from the bottom up." Now social historians were concerned with achieving a historical perspective on the everyday activities of ordinary people. All of a sudden the history of women, minorities, sports, labor, and other subjects became the focus of historians and the reading public. Many of these themes are then translated to the cinema and television where they are seen and become understood by millions.

Beginning in the seventeenth century, the people who settled Michigan's Upper Peninsula were often viewed negatively by the dominant culture. There were Native Americans who entered the region through Sault Ste. Marie. They were followed by French explorers, fur traders and missionaries. This situation remained constant through the eighteenth century with the transfer of the region to British and finally American control.

Then in the fourth decade of the nineteenth century, copper and iron were discovered by Douglass Houghton and William Burt respectively. The development of these rich and extensive mineral deposits needed a labor force which was not available locally. Soon after the news of these discoveries spread, Cornish, French Canadian, German, and Irish immigrants flocked to the Upper Peninsula. This began a grand migration of immigrants from around the world. The 1910 federal census shows there were 325,628 residents in the Upper Peninsula of which 124,034 or 26 percent were immigrants. In Marquette County there were 16,442 immigrants with 4,453 listed as miners or trammers. Thus some 44 percent of the immigrant population was engaged in these two aspects of mining, while even more were working at mine sites in different capacities. There were twenty nationalities represented on the Marquette Iron Range. Of these there were 2,117 Finns (48%) and in descending order: 797 English and Cornish, 732 Italians, 418 Swedes, 120 Canadians and then the figures drop to double digits.

Although mining was so important to the economy and lives of the people of the Marquette Iron Range, few of the miners had the time or inclination to write of their experiences above or below ground. The histories of iron mining that we have are primarily company histories which provide one side of the experience.

A few miners' accounts exist, but unfortunately most of them remain unpublished and consigned to archival files and family records. In the central Upper Peninsula, there are numerous oral interviews at the Central Upper Peninsula and University Archives on the campus of Northern Michigan University, which chronicle the lives of miners.

Publishing autobiographies is difficult and many of these publications are privately published and have limited distribution. As a result there are few accounts of the story of what actually happened in the mine or history "from the bottom up."

Fortunately in the latter half of the twentieth century, retired miners have had the time and inclination to write about their experiences in and about the mines. In 1987, just prior to his death, Thurston S. Jenkins wrote about his experiences in Ishpeming's Holmes Mine operated by Cleveland Cliffs between 1926 and 1928. He worked there for a short period of time and then moved to

Flint, Michigan and a new work experience.[1] A few years later Levi Etelmaki published two autobiographical works, The Blue Collar Aristocracy and Many Shadows, Many Voices. Both of these works deal with mining and life in Negaunee.[2]

The students at National Mine and now the Aspen Ridge Schools have produced a series of studies of local communities which have been published under the title, Red Dust, beginning in 1983. In 1994 the issue of Red Dust focused on the sesquicentennial of iron ore discovery in 1844 and was dedicated to mining. The students included interviews with many miners. In the same year, Elizabeth Morrissey's eighth grade English classes at Gwinn Middle School produced a booklet called Men of Steel. This work was also based on oral interviews with former miners.[3]

Social historians and the general public are pleased to see the publication of the Ronn autobiographical monograph. Ernie's account provides us with a few of what it was like to grow up on Negaunee's Ann Street and then become a miner with its attendant

---

[1]Thurston S. Jenkins. The Days of Mines. Naperville, IL: William Jenkins, 1990.

[2]Levi Etelmaki. The Blue Collar Aristocracy. Escanaba: Richard's Printing, 1997; Many Shadows, Many Voices. Privately published, 1998.

[3]The annual booklets, Red Dust can be found in most local libraries. See: Red Dust National Mine, MI: National Mine School, 1994; Josh Peterson, Kristie Usher, Chad Sherman, and Guy Viviano, eds. Men of Steel. Gwinn: Privately published, c1994.

hardships, fears, colorful characters and tales, hopes and dreams. This is a historical study "from the bottom up" those fifty-two steps by a person who was an eyewitness.

Russell M. Magnaghi
Northern Michigan University
Director, Center for Upper Peninsula Studies
October 12, 2000.

Acknowledgements

Over the years organizations and individuals have had their hand in getting this work published. From the onset, I would personally thank the United Steel Workers of America, Cleveland Cliffs Iron Company, and the miners for accepting me. They were the ones who initially made this work possible.

Then there are those people who encouraged me to write this story for future generations. Burt Boyum was one of the most persistent, urging me to "tell it like you see it." Ellwood Mattson and Dr. Don Elzinga actively promoted the project from the beginning.

Publication of a book is a major undertaking. Dr. Michael Marsden, former Dean of the College of Arts and Sciences at Northern Michigan University and director of the Northern Michigan University Press, first saw the value of this work and promoted its publication. Dr. Russell Magnaghi, director of the Center for Upper Peninsula Studies, took the necessary steps to get the work prepared for publication and then published.

I am grateful to the many individuals who prepared the manuscript for the printer. Shirley Mattson and Mary Stone took my scribblings, deciphered and typed them, all the while urging me "to keep going." From Iron Mountain, Dixie Franklin provided her editorial expertise to the process as did Michelle Kangas of Ishpeming (who had worked in the Tilden Mine) and Dr. Magnaghi of Northern Michigan University. Through the process, Sue Ann Salo and Patty Healey provided critical secretarial assistance.

Besides the words, there were the graphics which needed the assistance of other individuals. The cover was created by Northern Michigan University student Susie Aston. Gil Dawe helped me develop the mine diagrams and Bobbi Gurnoe added the artistic touch. Jim Godell took photographs of me at the Negaunee Mine site and Tom Buchkoe preserved old photographs used in the study. Curator Kaye Hiebel at the Marquette County Historical Society was helpful in finding additional photographs for the study. Len Warmanen and Martha Stott also provided me with photographs. The map of Ann Street was developed by Pat Farrell. Don Ryan and Dale Hemmila of Cleveland Cliffs Iron Company found photographs and provided me with other courtesies. I also want to acknowledge the financial assistance provided by the United Steelworkers of America, Local 4950, of Negaunee.

Finally, there were many readers like Jim Carter who offered insights and Suzan Travis-Robyns who proofread the work on its way to the publisher. Without these individuals and others who might go unmentioned, this monograph would have never reached the publisher and to all of them a hearty thanks. However, in the end, this is my work and I am responsible for any errors that might be found.

Chapter 1—Ann Street

I shall never forget my first shift at the Negaunee Mine on the midnight shift of June 22, 1943. Although I had lived all my life between two mines, and lived among many miners (my father, grandfather and many uncles had worked in the mines for many years), and brought lunch pails to the miners, I still wondered what awaited me underground.

No one knows or understands what went through the minds of the early immigrant miners as they stood near the shaft waiting to go underground for the first time. I believe that among the worries and concerns included what they would see, what was to be expected of them, how were they going to do the work that they had no knowledge of, how they would communicate with a boss or fellow worker who didn't speak or understand their language, and how much light would be given by the candle or carbide lamp they carried on their heads? Not only were these the worries of the miner, but worries shared by his family that watched him go to the mine for the first time. And even though the men in my family had gone underground before me, these are the things I felt as I waited to go underground.

From the early days, the mines attracted men of many nationalities. As new mines were developed, the need for more miners grew. Some came alone and later returned to their homelands and brought their families. Others came with their families and were determined to remain here at any cost.

These immigrants not only mined our iron ore, but also gave us the benefit of their many skills and crafts. They gave us the fine foods and their knowledge of making wine, moonshine and beer common to their countries. Food was important to most miners; not food for dieting, but the hearty foods of working people.

Waiting to go underground, I recalled the many versions and Chippewa Indian interpretations of names for Negaunee and nearby Ishpeming. The most frequent translation that I remember was that Ishpeming meant heaven and Negaunee meant hell.

My father was born in Ishpeming and my mother, who was born in Finland, came to Negaunee where she lived the rest of her life. A Finnish legend involves the Finns who lived in the Savo area of Finland. My maternal grandparents and mother from that region are "Savvolinen." Legend has it that all Savvolinens are wild people, so wild that one could tame the wildest wolf two days sooner than one could tame a Savvolinen.

With this background of being born of parents from "heaven" and "hell" and considered wilder than a wolf, it is fitting and fortunate that I lived the first fifty years of my life on Ann Street in Negaunee. The street had few equals and will always be my favorite. The street ran south and parallel to the main railroad lines into Negaunee and Ishpeming (now parallel to County Road 480 East). These tracks carried the old coal-fired steam engines with their ore cars, freight, and passenger cars. Empty ore cars were brought to the mines to be loaded with ore, and returned to the Marquette ore docks on Lake Superior for loading on Great Lakes ore carriers. Coal for the big boilers at the mines and power plants also had to come along these tracks.

Passengers between Ishpeming and Chicago rode the Chicago North Western Railway. When the railroad company replaced the coal-fired steam engine with the sleek and shining "400" steamliner, all thought it would be the ultimate in passenger service for all time. It could make a round trip between Ishpeming and Chicago every day. It began its eight-hour trip or 400 plus minutes to Chicago by leaving Ishpeming around 7:00 a.m. The 400 would be back in Ishpeming at midnight, and turn around for the next trip a few hours later. These tracks separated the people of Ann Street from the better class living on the opposite side, according to some people.

For my first five years, my world was mostly confined to the thirty-one houses between the Big Hill and Maki's Hill, approximately five blocks east. Every one of these houses was within 200 feet of the Athens and

Negaunee mines. The Rintimaki and Vaisinen families lived in a house only fifty feet from the Athens Mine shaft. I doubt whether any other house was ever built as close. Other houses were even closer to the railroad tracks that led into the mine along the ore stockpile.

With the exception of one house, all were owned by the mining companies. Thirteen of the company-owned houses had two families living in them. Every family had one or more active miners, or former miners who left the mines because of age, health, or injury. Monthly rent for each family ranged from five dollars to thirteen dollars. Electricity and water averaged another three dollars to five dollars per month.

The landlord provided some maintenance for the interior on an irregular schedule, usually a two-year schedule. Only one room could be remodeled at a time. The renter had to choose one of two available options. He could purchase the needed paint or wallpaper, and the mining company would provide the labor. If he elected to do the work or hire someone, the landlord paid for all the supplies. Most elected to have the paint and paper purchased by the company, as there were always two neighbors who would do all the labor for two dollars to five dollars, depending on the room size.

The only other maintenance provided was a periodic chimney cleaning. Every house had two chimneys. In the two-family buildings, each chimney had two stoves connected to it. Every family had a wood-burning kitchen stove and a larger stove for heating.

According to my grandfather, many of the houses had additions put on after they were originally built. The house I lived in had four rooms added in 1902. Two more rooms were added to each floor, along with an open porch.

Lots were fifty by one hundred feet. Most had two-story barns and an outhouse, in addition to the house. The barns were partitioned so that each family had a place to store winter fuel and to shelter their cows. Because of the limited size of the lots, there was no way of relocating an outhouse if the hole underneath was full. This meant that the outhouse would be built in a corner of the lot on the alley side, and the hole underneath dug deep to avoid any possibility of it ever filling up. All outhouses have one thing in common. In the summer they are too close to the house, and in the winter they are too far.

Those who have had experience with an outhouse are aware of the cold, and the times when snow covered the seats because of a storm. They do not forget how the distance between the floor and seat shrunk during the winter. Snow brought in on shoes or boots builds up to where the knees come up near the chin when sitting. It was not the widely advertised toilet paper of today that was used. Sears Roebuck, Montgomery Ward, and Spiegel catalogs provided this necessity. Twisting and crumpling the pages of catalogs still did not make them anywhere comparable to Charmin, White Cloud, or Soft Touch. At best, the pages were more like sheets of forty-grit sandpaper than any brand. These outhouses were favorite targets for Halloween pranksters. The height of outhouses and their narrow width made them very easy to tip over.

One incident involving our outhouse was never forgotten by my father. One day a young neighbor girl came out of the house crying because her kitten had somehow fallen down into the outhouse. Because of the depth of the hole, the only way my father could think of to affect a rescue was to lower a pole down to the cat. He grabbed a clothesline prop and extended it down into the hole. Although the prop was over seven feet long, it didn't reach the kitten. Holding one end of the prop, he extended his arm further into the hole, and hoped the kitten would grab on and climb out. Little did he realize that when the scared little kitten got onto the prop, it wouldn't take long for it to come out of its prison. Not only did it scamper up the prop, but also over my father's arm and shoulder, down his back and over the seat of his pants. Once out into the open, the frightened kitten ran away. Had my father gotten hold of that cat, whatever remained of its nine lives would have come to a quick ending.

The company-owned houses lacked any insulation in the walls, attics or floors. Limited electric wiring provided lighting. Only a single porcelain or brass bulb-holder hung down in the center of the room. To turn the lights on or off, there was a pull chain or small switch on the fixture. The wiring was installed with two separate wires, one ground and one live wire. Fuse boxes were limited to only two or three circuits. Overloading caused many burnt-out fuses that could be fixed by placing a copper penny between the burnt fuse and the contact in the fuse box. There were no basements in many houses until later years. Small dugouts, much like a root cellar, were dug underneath the house. Potatoes could be stored in this small space. Access to the cellar was through a door cut into the floor above this space. Usually the door was in the middle of the kitchen. The linoleum was carefully folded over to expose the door for entry.

Because the houses had only board skirting between the ground and building, it made for drafty floors and provided easy entry into the house for both mice and rats. As a young kid, whenever I went to get potatoes, it was a scary adventure. With only a flashlight or candle, I envisioned rats lurking everywhere. The shadows cast by spider webs didn't lessen the scare.

In the winter, every house would have large icicles hanging from the eaves because of heat loss. The lack of insulation also meant that the temperature in the house would drop as the fire in the stove went down. Getting out of bed to put more fuel in the stove was the only way to keep the house warm and water pipes from freezing. On the coldest mornings, school clothes would be put on top of the stove or hung on chairs nearby to warm up. Many times, I stood near the heat of the stove to keep myself warm.

For many years, the only indoor plumbing was a single galvanized pipe to the kitchen sink. Whenever possible, tenants built a drain board between the sink and wall. The sink, mounted on brackets to the wall, was open underneath. A homemade curtain was often hung on a rope to conceal the soaps stored there.

When the landlord finally decided to put in an indoor toilet, it was more of an afterthought without planning. In our house, the toilet was put under the upstairs stairway. Crowded into this small space, a four-foot clothes pole or pipe was mounted between the stair runner and wall. It was more than enough to hang the limited clothes of the family.

Partial or full basements were ultimately dug under the houses, making the floor above warmer, more difficult for the rats to get in, and better storage for potatoes and other vegetables.

These houses, absent of either a shower or bathtub, made it necessary to find alternate means of taking a bath. Before reaching school age, the galvanized clothes tub served as a bathtub. Water heated in pots on the kitchen stove was the only means of providing warm water to bathe in.

Later, my close friend Art Maki and I usually went to the Athens Mine for a shower. On Sunday evenings, we would go to the mine dry house to clean up for school the next day. How leisurely we could shower depended on the mine watchman on duty. If Jim Blee or Frank Champaign was on, we had all the time necessary. They would caution us not to get burned by the hot water, and often even sat down in the dry or on outside benches and talked with us. If Lambert Chard was working, it was a different story. Depending on his mood, we were either given permission to hurry up and take our shower, or were chased away. Some of the women and girls also went to the mine for showers. For some reason, it seemed that Thursday night was the best time for them to go. They did not shower in the big shower room for miners, but in the much smaller shower room in the foreman's dry. There, they had privacy, as the room had doors that could be locked.

Many of the Finnish families with saunas provided the most often used method of bathing. I remember going with my grandparents to the Alvin Laitinen farm in Eagle Mills, the Herman Jarvi's and Simon Maki's on Ann Street, Herman Laitinen's in the Rolling Mill Location, and others. A public sauna was operating on Lincoln Street. One could go there for a dime. Whenever I went for a sauna with my grandparents, all of the host families had one thing in common: to even suggest paying for the privilege of taking a sauna would be an insult to the host. The table would be set and loaded with homemade bread, biscuits, cheese, meat and more. After taking a sauna, everyone sat and enjoyed the excellent food and conversation. Even after installation of showers and tubs in the company houses, the Finns still went to their friend's saunas on Saturday nights. This still remains a tradition.

Living across the avenue from my grandparents, I spent most of my time with them. According to my parents, I spoke mostly Finnish during my earliest years. I don't believe that any grandson could ever be closer than I was to my maternal grandparents. Unfortunately, I have no recollection of my paternal grandfather, and my paternal grandmother had moved to Superior soon after his death. Grandma Ronn was a quiet and pleasant lady and had a good sense of humor. I did have some opportunities to spend time with her.

My grandparents were Finn immigrants who brought with them the tastes of the Old Country. Dairy products are an important part of the Finn diet and milk is heavily consumed in Finland as a fresh whole beverage and as buttermilk. As a result fresh milk, buttermilk and butter were readily available to the family. Breads are the mainstay of the Finn diet. Traditionally interesting varieties of rye breads developed which are the absolute favorite of Finns. My grandma brought with her the art of making delicious sour rye bread. When she baked the rye bread and served it warm with fresh buttermilk and butter I was in heaven.

Whenever possible, I was either in the barn while the cows were being milked early in the morning and evening. While my grandparents lived in Negaunee, grandma did most of the milking and caring for the animals. Grandpa had no real love for the cows and had little time for them. Working in the mine, getting wood for winter, growing potatoes, and repairing shoes and boots took up almost all of his time.

Helping to get hay down to the cows, along with giving them water and feed, gave me the feeling of importance and pride in helping. Whether grandma looked upon all my efforts as helping or hindering, she would never say. Nothing that I did was ever criticized nor was I scolded by either of these grandparents. Neither could do anything wrong in my eyes.

Early Ventures to the Mine

From my uncle's yard, many times I watched Athens Mine miners going between the dry and tunnel leading to the cage. I got much closer when I was about ten years old. My father and grandfather worked as partners at the Negaunee Mine, and at that time the men had to come to surface to eat their lunch. During the hot days of summer I would carry their lunch buckets to them at lunchtime. Instead of having their lunch pails in the hot dry, it was better to bring a fresher lunch. It also gave me an opportunity to bring them a freshly made pasty or piece of pie.

Getting to the mine required a trip down and up the sandcut, over a narrow strip of land, and down the bottom to the shaft house. When the train was loading ore, I would wait until an empty car was spotted near the shovel and duck under the couplings between the railroad cars. Going under the trestle and the big sheave wheels between the shaft and engine room made it impossible not to get oil or iron ore on my clothes. Past the trestle and shaft, a flight of cement steps had to be climbed to get to the dry house. The long dry house was on the left and the engine house on the right side of the stairway.

Looking into the engine room, I could see the massive rope drums spinning as the cage and skips were moving up and down the mineshaft. The big wire cables made an eerie sound as they ran at high speed over the sheave wheels and on to the hoisting drums. At that time I didn't realize that these big wire ropes were also very long. They went from the engine house to the bottom of the shaft. Negaunee Mine had a depth of about 1,500 feet. Combined with the distance from the shaft to the hoist, overall it was over a half mile. The Athens Mine, almost double in depth, required cables more than three-quarters of a mile long.

A well-kept lawn with a steam pond in the middle was surrounded on three sides by the engine house, dry house and the main office. The steam pond had a number of small fountains that pushed the water high into the air. With the flowers surrounding the pond it made a pretty sight. As the miners sat on the long benches along the outside wall of the dry, they looked out at the lawn and fountain as they ate their lunch.

Sometimes I would walk past my father and grandfather, failing to recognize them because of their ore-covered faces and dirty clothes. All miners looked different than they did in street clothes. One thing they had in common was the look and expressions on their faces and in their eyes. Because of their dirty faces, the eyes had a haunting look. Not out of fear, but more of concern and worry and deep in thought. I will never forget looking at them and remembering their eyes.

I could speak and understand the Finnish language and often talked with the old Finn miners. As they sat for their lunches they more or less separated into groups of Finns, Swedes, Italians and Frenchmen. This gave them an opportunity to better communicate in their native language. The men came from every part of Negaunee, surrounding areas and other towns, and one could not tell which "side of the track they came from."

As time passed, I was often teased by and talked to by these dirt-covered men. Most knew enough English to give them a chance to talk to this kid who spoke such good Finn. Seldom could I leave the mine without a miner reaching out with a piece of homemade pastry or piece of candy in his hand. I am convinced that the wife had been told to put a little extra in the lunch pail only for my benefit.

As I waited for the empty lunch pails, I could walk through the dirty and clean clothes ends of the dry. With the exception of a small room with a couple of shower heads, the miners had to wash up after the end of the shift in small wash basins that were placed on a long shelf. The shelf ran the length of a wide, long sink, with many hot and cold-water taps spaced along the sink. The miner would put water in a basin and do his best to get the ore off his body. It was easy to identify a miner coming from the mines by the dark ore rings around his eyes, hairline and hands.

At the south end of the dry there was a small room where rolls of white blasting fuses hung. Blasting caps were stored on a shelf. This is the room where a fuse cutter would carefully measure the fuse into eight-foot lengths and crimp a blasting cap to one end. A string would be looped above the cap to wrap around the stick of dynamite in which a cap would be pushed by the miner just before charging the holes to be blasted. The ready capped fuses would be bundled with 10, 15 or 20 fuses per bundle and put into a special fuse can. Each of the round metal cans had a leather strap to hold the cover down and a rubber hose long enough to carry over the shoulder. Cans were identified with the same contract number as the miner.

Next to the fuse shack, a long flight of concrete steps went down to the tunnel leading to the cage and out to the timber field and shops. When it came time for the men to go back into the mine, I watched from the open door of the engine house as they filed by with their refilled water jugs to complete the last half of their shift. Each man turned and looked out before going onto the stairway and back underground.

Chapter 2—Negaunee, A Mining Town

Negaunee, and all of the immediate surrounding area, was a community of people with wide differences in nationality, customs, and religious convictions among other things. This area was much like the beautiful patchwork quilts the women made out of old clothing, taking the best and most colorful pieces of cloth. They would cut, sew, and after hours and hours of working together in a quilting bee, the final product was a beautiful, colorful and long-lasting patchwork quilt. The people of that bygone era were just as colorful and diversified as the quilts they made. They also joined together and using the best of what they had, created a way of life that was as colorful as a quilt. Just like the hard-working quilters who cut, fitted, and sewed the patches together, the people demonstrated equal patience and determination and made a quilt of life that held the community together.

Another word for a quilt is comforter. While the ladies made their patchwork comforter, another comforter was being made. Using the best they had, the community joined together and made a way of life that gave a higher degree of comfort to all, lasted throughout their lifetime, and presented future generations with a pattern to continue making the public comforter better for everyone. History, yet to be made, will only prove whether we have the same degree of tolerance, patience, and determination of our forebearers. The best we can hope for is to somehow come close or to equal their unselfish contribution to life itself. To better their record, I fear is impossible.

Businesses

Unfortunately, I cannot remember each and every business of my youth and I apologize for any oversight. All of them were good people and without their patience, understanding and support, one can only speculate what the lives and futures of the early miners might have been.

With few exceptions, most of Negaunee business owners and operators were family-people. Many were organized by men who had worked in the area mines. The exceptions were stores like the A&P and the Co-operative store.

Many stores and professional offices had a common family name. The Thomas name appeared on at least three grocery stores, a plumbing and heating establishment, and on the door of a dentist. Another family name was the Collins family. At least three grocery stores bore this family name. The Perala family owned and operated a hardware store, and a funeral home that still bears the Perala name. In addition to Perala Hardware, there was the Sawbridge Hardware on the west end of Iron Street and Arvid Nyland had his hardware store on Jackson Street. Other family names were the Levines, Lowensteins and Wehmanen families that had clothing stores. The Wehmanen family, also had a jewelry store where father and son repaired and sold watches, silver, and other gifts.

Some of the other business places that I remember well were the grocery stores of Selim Mattson, Winter and Suess, Lindberg, Dighera, Fred Ollila and his son Paul, "Porky" Robare, and "Guzzy" Holman. Most grocery stores made home delivery, some both morning and afternoon deliveries. One of the most popular and friendly teamsters was "Lefty" Lenten who worked at the T.L. Collins store on Jackson Street. Lefty was our regular teamster for many years. He always had a smile on his face and was friendly to those who he brought groceries to. This made him a friend of all.

A long-time butcher and manager of this same store was "Tip" Alongo. Tip was a valuable asset to his employer because of his ability to talk to many customers in their native Finnish language. Tip never forgot the run-in he got into with Senja Hokanen. Upon arriving from Finland, Senja and her husband Mikko first came to live on Ann Street. Though good and steady customers of the store, this relationship came very close to ending as a result of one particular delivery to the Hokanen home.

Early one morning Senja stormed into the store, waving a piece of paper and raising all kinds of hell to Tip. The startled Tip asked what was troubling her. As she continued waving the paper, she said, "My Mikko always pays his bills on time and why did you have to threaten him?" Tip asked to see the paper she was waving in his face. She handed it to him and continued her tirade. The only markings on the paper were the letters P.M., to advise the teamster that the groceries were to be delivered in the afternoon. Senja had a different reading that apparently caused her a sleepless night. She read the letters as a warning: "Pay, Mikko". Finally, she was satisfied with the explanation given and returned home happy and content that her Mikko's integrity wasn't damaged.

Operating service stations were men like Walt Neely, Adolph Violetta, Ted Smedman, Lloyd Anderson, Ernie La Cosse, and Percy Dotson. At one time you could drive into these service stations and get real service. Gas cost nineteen or twenty cents a gallon. Windshield and windows would be washed, oil and radiator checked, and tires checked upon request. All of these services were performed while the owners sat in their cars. Before leaving the station one always heard, "Thank you. Come again," — a statement of appreciation for your patronage.

Car dealers like Abe Wolfe, Wilfred Hill, Curtis Donnethorne sold cars and repaired them. Others like Paul Honkavaara and his sons operated their garage next to the fire hall. For years, Art Samuelson had his tire sales and vulcanizing shop on Iron Street.

Kids could go to many places to enjoy ice cream, fountain drinks, malts, and sodas. There was the chocolate shop, Arnetts Drug Store, Cronin's Drug Store, and Oscar Kultalahti's small store next to the A&P on the east end of Iron Street.

Oscar, a short stocky Finn, who lived on Ann Street's lower end, ran a store that was a favorite of the kids. He had the long candy counter filled with penny and nickel candy. The ice cream freezer and the malted milk machines were located at the front of his little store.

For fifteen cents Oscar would make different flavored malts that filled the metal container of the mixer.

During one election, Oscar tossed his hat in the political ring and sought the nomination for sheriff of Marquette County. As a Finn, Oscar felt confident that he would get the support of the majority of Finnish voters. With a big vote from the Finns, other voters from different areas would give him victory. His confidence of winning ended as the votes were counted. Though not certain, I believe his total vote countywide was less than one hundred, and the number seventy-eight comes to mind. Oscar didn't carry the Finn vote in the Fifth Ward. Had the kids who knew Oscar and patronized his store voted, the vote might well have given him the victory he sought.

A number of restaurants provided good meals in Negaunee. Among the early ones were the Main Drift, operated by the Laiho family, the Negaunee Cafe, and Hillbilly Restaurant. Two family-operated bakery shops made breads and other baked goods, as good as any bakery, better than many. Torreano's Bakery on Jackson Street was popular for its Italian bread and hard rolls. The Kompsi family, for a number of years, had its shop on the County Road. They made an excellent rye bread and coffee bread, both favorites of the Finnish and other Scandinavian people.

On the west end of Iron Street, the Violetta family operated the Viga Bowling Alley, and later a music store that sold musical instruments and records. These were two of the three business places that bore the Violetta name.

Whatever the needs for home maintenance of heating or plumbing were available at Warner Heating and Plumbing, or Thomas Heating and Plumbing. Electrical work and supplies were available at Wangberg Electric owned by Fritz Wangberg. He was joined by his son, Keith. This business ran for many years. Alex Guizzetti and his employees installed terrazzo floors in many buildings throughout the area. While these merchants provided the basic needs for the people, others made their contributions to their security and protection.

Men and boys had a number of barber shops in town for their haircuts. There was Remillard's shop on Gold Street, Honka's in the basement of the A&P store, Duquette's Barber Shop, Bruno Lehto on Iron Street, and Langsford's Barber Shop in the Railo Building. Women and girls had at least two beauty shops where all of their beauty needs were available. I do not remember the names of these shops, but they were located on Iron Street. There were a number of men and women who cut hair and gave home care for the ladies, men, and children.

The Maki Studio, in the center of Iron Street, took family pictures, wedding pictures, graduation pictures, and such for the people in the area. Waino Maki, the photographer and developer of pictures, was very skilled.

The Bannon Cleaners had their business on the western end of Iron Street. Clothes could be brought in or picked up for laundering or dry cleaning. A jovial Irishman, John McNamara, managed the place for years. Better known as "Piggy," he also held the office of County Chairman of the Democratic Party. This position had a close relationship to the miners.

Not far from Bannon Cleaners on the other side of the street, Jimmy Miller had his newsstand. At Miller News, magazines and a variety of out of area newspapers were available. Jim had the equivalent of what we now call a convenience store. He carried a variety of lunch meats, canned goods, beer and wine, candy, pop, and other products.

Further on the eastern end of Iron Street, the Pellow family ran its Pellow Printing business. In addition to wedding announcements, election ballots, and similar items, it also published the Iron Herald, Negaunee's own newspaper.

The second employer with the largest number of workers was at the factory located on Iron Street near Bannon Cleaners. I am not sure of its primary product, but believe it was women's gloves. Whatever its products, a number of women worked at this factory prior to its closing.

All types of insurance were sold by the Negaunee Agency and the Tamblyn Insurance Agency. There was another plumbing and heating firm in Negaunee operated by a family of the same name as the insurance company, presumably by the same Tamblyn's.

There were two individuals who had small shops on Iron Street, one repaired shoes and boots in his shoe repair shop near Pellow Printing. Across the street was a tailor shop where one could get a tailor-made suit or clothes altered.

Standing on the east end of Iron Street was the Breitung Hotel, one of the area's best at one time. I believe there was a second and smaller hotel behind the Winter and Suess store. I know there was a bar, the Hotel Bar, in the basement of this building.

The Cleveland Cliffs Iron Company had its land department in Negaunee in the building that now serves as the Negaunee Public School Administrative offices. The First National Bank of Negaunee has been in continuous operation for almost the same length of time as the City of Negaunee was founded. With both a public school system and the St. Paul School, parents had a choice of sending their children to either the Catholic school or the public school.

Within the business community were a five-and-ten store and a variety store. Both sold such items as wool yarn, thread, needles, buttons, and patterns. Small toys and trinkets could be purchased at the lowest prices in these stores.

Professions

Two well-known attorneys practiced law in Negaunee: Aaron Lowenstein, who was a member of the family that operated the clothing store, and Mike DeFant. Mike contributed much time and effort on behalf of the miners during their union organizing campaign. We will always remember his work on behalf of the miners.

Medical and dental services were available from many sources. The dentists that I recall are Doctors Sanregret, Bessolo, Whale, Nankervis, and Thomas. Negaunee has had a number of medical doctors that were respected by the people. I recall Doctors Mudge, McIntyre, and Gulickson who worked and had offices at the Negaunee Dispensary. Dr. Burke was another of the old-time doctors. These doctors and others treated patients at home, the Ishpeming Hospital, and the Twin City Hospital in Negaunee.

Of all of these doctors I was most familiar with Dr. William A. Mudge. It was he who delivered me in 1925. An older aunt was also brought into the world by Dr. Mudge. During his long and distinguished career, he delivered countless babies and had a long list of patients, including all of the Cleveland Cliffs miners and their families in Negaunee and outlying areas. Miners paid a monthly premium for medical care. It cost one dollar a month for the single men and two dollars for the miners with families.

What is now the Masonic Lodge on Teal Lake Avenue was originally the Negaunee Dispensary. The doctors parked their cars on the south side of the dispensary. To get into the building, they had to walk through a room about ten by twelve feet. This was also the clinic where cuts might be stitched, plaster casts put on broken legs and arms, and where miners routinely had the ore in their ears flushed out.

Another room of about the same size as the clinic was in the northwest corner of the building. Large bottles and containers were stacked on shelves behind a wooden wall with a service window. The medicine prescribed by the doctor was usually available without the need to go to a drug store.

In the center of the first floor was a large waiting room. Three doctors offices and examining rooms opened into the large room. Patients sat on wooden benches and chairs waiting their turn to see their doctor. The next patient to get into the doctor's office was the one sitting in the closest chair by his door. As each patient came into the waiting room, they knew the patients ahead of them. Each waited until one of the earlier arrivals went to sit on the chair next to their doctor's door. He would move to the chair, knowing that he was the next to get into his doctor's office. It is remarkable to look back and realize that there was no receptionist, office clerk, or accounting department anywhere in the dispensary. Obviously all of this record keeping and other clerical work was done by the doctors.

These early doctors worked long hours that few modern medical providers work. Dr. Mudge had office hours at the Dispensary from 8 to 9 a.m., 1 to 2 p.m. and 7 to 8 p.m. every day Monday through Friday. Saturday mornings and afternoons he would have the same hours as during the week. In between these hours he would go to the Twin City and Ishpeming Hospitals to check on his patients, including injured miners. He had a regular schedule of performing non-emergency surgery at the hospitals.

Emergencies often interrupted his daily routine. A common sight was to see his Chrysler sedan parked in front of homes where he would be caring for the homebound, sick and injured. Often he would be seeing people late at night before ending his work for that day. His wife of many years often rode with him and waited in the car as he made his rounds. This must have been one of the few opportunities they had to be together because of his long hours.

I recall one Friday night when I went to see him for some health reason. As I was his last patient, he said, "Sit awhile and let's talk." Sometime before that visit, the mining company had made the decision to close the dispensary and sell it. Dr. Mudge was denied the opportunity to buy the building that he had been associated with for such a long time.

Determined to continue serving his patients, he had an addition built to his home, which was right next to the old dispensary. As he told me of this, he was looking out the window at the wall of the dispensary, wondering why any young doctor was given a chance denied him. I

18

am sure that the old doctor was hurt and troubled by this. As we sat, he reminisced about his childhood and how, during the hard and difficult times, the family had to rely and live on one or two meals of oatmeal every day. Though some thought of him as a wealthy man, he was not. He had lived a fairly comfortable life and raised two boys who followed their father into the medical profession. His home or lifestyle was not pretentious nor did he ever portray himself as anything but a kind and considerate man caring for those in need. Without his little black medical bag, strangers would have a difficult time identifying him as a doctor.

Many of the thousands of babies he delivered in his early years and the services he gave to the injured or sick were never paid in money. The absence of insurance and the level of earnings in the mines made any payment with money difficult and perhaps impossible. However, he told me that many who couldn't pay their bills made sincere efforts to meet their obligations in other ways. Those living on the small farms surrounding Negaunee would bring vegetables and apples in the fall. When a cow or pig was butchered, they brought fresh meat. Hunters and fishermen shared their game with Dr. Mudge.

Dr. Mudge once told me that in the early and mid-1940's when the United Steelworkers of America was conducting an organizing drive among employees of area mining companies, he had been misled. He said he was one of those who had listened and followed the union-haters and their attacks against the miners and the union they sought. He told about the many times he had heard their conversations and the special radio broadcast condemning and predicting the end of the mining industry and how Ishpeming and Negaunee would become ghost towns if the union succeeded.

How wrong and how foolish he said he had been to listen to these people. He looked at me and said, "I've known you since the day I brought you into this world. I have known your family and so many others like you I have known you better than to ever believe that you and others involved in the campaign were anything like the charges being brought up against you." He finished by shaking my hand and saying that the United Steelworkers Union was the best thing that ever happened to the men in the mines and to our community.

I have never forgotten that night's talk with the doctor and his contribution to the people. In retrospect, one of my deepest regrets is that I didn't tell this fine man on behalf of all of the striking miners and their friends, "Thank God for Dr. Mudge."

Very late in his practice and shortly before his death, Dr. Mudge had a bad case of the flu. Unable to go the short distance to the drug store, he had called in a prescription for himself. Joe Mautino, the druggist, asked me if I was going past the doctor's house on my way home. He told me of Dr. Mudge's call for medicine and I told Joe that whatever my plans were, it was more important to get the medicine delivered. The doctor answered the door dressed in pajamas and a heavy bathrobe. He looked very sick. He could not remember any time in the past when he was so sick and unable to see any patients for three days. As I gave him the bag of medicine, I asked if I wasn't doing something no other person had done before—that I was bringing him medicine instead of him giving medicine to others as he had done thousands of times.

Dr. Mudge and his wife both died within a day or so of each other. Negaunee and all those who knew them suffered a loss of two very nice people who would have been an asset to any community. His memory will last forever among those of us who knew him. After his passing, his two sons Tom and William continued the family name in medicine, delivering the same high quality of care and compassion for their patients. It is ironic that Dr. Mudge Sr. delivered me in June of 1925 at the Ishpeming Hospital. In January of 1970 his son Tom performed major surgery on my father and gave him one more year of life in relative comfort.

Another well-known figure in the medical field was Nurse Akins. She was a nurse who visited the homes of those recuperating from surgery, and to check up and care for those confined to their homes. She was easily identified in her white uniform carrying a medical bag, and driving a dark coupe. A woman of considerable strength, she was considered as rough by many.

Equally divided between caring for the sick was her dedication and active work on behalf of the Women's Christian Temperance Union (WCTU). As a member of the WCTU, she never hesitated to preach their opposition to drinking alcohol. Constant in her expression of opposition to any and all liquor consumption, she became even more involved when the issue of permitting taverns to be open and to sell liquor on Sunday afternoons was put to a vote by the people. Her loyalty and unyielding support of the WCTU position was not enough to defeat the proposal and the new hours came into effect.

From these memories of the merchants and professional people, one can get a picture of life in Negaunee some sixty years ago. The population of Negaunee may have been somewhere between 6,000 and 7,000. It was a bustling town that provided most of the needs for the people in Negaunee and the surrounding areas of Eagle Mills, Midway and Suomi locations, Palmer and the North Country.

Fraternal Organizations

There were many different nationalities and groups who had their private lodges and clubs. The Finns had their Knights of Kaleva. At one time they had a large hall on Healy Avenue next to Lindberg's store where they held dances and other events. Over the years the famous and world renowned accordionist Viola Turpinen played at the Kaleva Hall. The Knights of Columbus had their private quarters, as did other similar groups. The big Osterbotten Hall on Teal Lake Avenue was the site of many weddings and dances. Just behind the Breitung Hotel was another large building where many wrestling and boxing matches were scheduled. This building was called either the Delpha Rink or Adelpha Rink, but in any event, well-known champions in these two sports did appear at this rink.

Taverns, Bars and Home Brew

The one segment that I have left out up to now is the role that the many taverns, bars, package liquor stores, home brewers, wine makers and moon shiners played in that bygone era. Left out of the family-owned businesses was another family that played a big part in the life of the beer parlors and beer drinkers. The three Lee Brothers, Roy, Hungary and Pug, operated a beer distributing warehouse, drove the school bus for the Negaunee Public Schools and had a moving company. All operated out of their warehouse on Healy Avenue. Not only did they provide keg and bottled beer to the licensed taverns, individuals could buy kegs of beer directly from the warehouse for private parties or any reason to celebrate. Their primary product in the early years was to wholesale Rahr Beer out of a brewery in Green Bay.

Early surveys indicate that at one time there were twenty-six legally licensed outlets for liquor within the city limits. How many unlicensed places was never reported or really known. These establishments outnumbered the churches in town by five-to-one. The churches seldom filled to capacity except for the holidays of Easter, Christmas and New Year's Eve. The bars and taverns were filled to capacity much more often, and I believe served much of the same purpose. Many sought comfort and an easing of stress or even fear in their respective places of worship. Others sought the same kind of relief from identical stress and pressure inside of their favorite bar or tavern. In a strange but understandable way, both church and tavern met the needs of their people. Who can say with certainty if Negaunee or the mining industry itself could have survived without both the churches and the bars of that time.

Like many other business establishments, many bars were family operations and some carried the family name. Gus Makela owned Makela's Bar. Across the street was Paris' Bar, owned by Rose Paris, Chris Johnson had his tavern, Vic Tamietti had Vic's Tavern. Vic

22

Palomaki had a tavern. I believe that at one time the Hotel Bar and Tony's Bar were owned by a Guizzetti family. I don't know whether they were from the same family or not. The Olympic Bar was operated by many generations of the Lafkas family. For a long time, "Fat" Ruona was the friendly operator of Swan's Tavern. "Cullie" Nassi ran the Manhattan Bar across the street from Swans. There were many other places where liquor could be legally sold, and were of equal importance and excitement. These are the ones that were most involved in my recollections of the past, and later when I became of age to patronize the licensed bars.

There were no comparable places to the taverns where the language, stories and life experiences could be heard. The taverns were also a source of immediate news when it involved the mines or the men. News of bad accidents spread throughout the bars soon after they occurred. Whenever certain levels of earnings were reached at any mine that also spread. Such benchmarks as the ten-dollar day, and pay of a dollar and a half and two dollar an hour were talked about.

When five dollars an hour was reached, it was proudly believed that the miners now had reached the highest possible level of wages. Not only were the miners' earnings of interest, but what they had done to earn them. The names of the miners, the mines and their output were soon well known. As each new level of miner's wages was reached, so too was their output that brought the higher earnings. This provided an area of comparison between mine and miners when there was a dispute over incentive earnings.

I don't believe that there ever was any other place than the taverns where one could listen and learn of the lifestyle of many of the old miners. It was within these walls where all of the people looked upon each other as equals. They did not pretend to be anything but themselves. They were people who were doing their best with what they had, providing for their family, living as friends and helpful neighbors and doing their best to make

23

the lives of those who came after them just a little more secure, safe and enjoyable.

It was not only the iron ore miners who brought their humor and stories into the bars, but also the lumberjacks from nearby logging camps and a few real characters who lived their lives differently.

Many stories could be told by those who visited the illegal establishments of the time. Those who made the moonshine, home brew and wine had their regular visitors; those visitors provided the same atmosphere for earthy conversation. The Blind Pigs, where liquor was sold during illegal hours and without license, along with a whorehouse or two, provided similar opportunities to talk.

One character that may not have been known throughout Negaunee was a recluse by the name of Jack Zuligger. The people on Ann Street and in the Eagle Mills area were familiar with this tall man. Little was known of his background or of his life in a small camp in the woods somewhere in Eagle Mills. What we knew of Jack was his periodic trips to town that took him along Ann Street.

As he walked toward town, he spoke very little to anyone. He was usually dressed in an old tattered dress suit, perhaps his best clothes to be worn in public. Though silent on the way to his favorite bar, his return trip was quite different. He would come down the street, doing a little jig as he staggered along, talking to himself in language and words that nobody understood. Jack was in a world of his own as he went through these actions walking the five miles home.

Fifty odd years after seeing this man, I was again reminded of him when I turned on the TV early one Sunday morning. This self-styled apostle using the electronic pulpit used gestures much like the drunken Jack Zuligger. After condemning everyone from the Pope to Mother Theresa, he would fall to his knees, wailing like a dying calf in a rainstorm and speaking in "tongues" coming directly to him from above. This performance ended with the plea for more and more gifts to his church, the only salvation, to those who believed only as he did.

24

The old hermit, even in his drunken state, knew better than to preach the same fire and brimstone threats of this particular and self-claimed messenger of Jesus, even though he danced a similar jig and spoke in his private tongue, from wherever it came.

Jack was reportedly an excellent woodcutter, making winter's wood for himself and the few friends he had nearby. He was an expert in sharpening all kinds of saws—bucksaw, crosscut and especially the large circular blades used on buzz saws.

Hanging One On

Another old man who made his trips to town on a fairly regular schedule was Heikki Harju, a hard-working miner who had lost his wife and remained single after her death. Heikki never had a car. He would walk to town and back unless picked up by a neighbor. On one hot Saturday night, Heikki went to town solely for the purpose of "hanging one on." Try as he did, he was unable to make a stop in every tavern on Iron Street. The last tavern between him and home was Chris Johnson's. As he came to the tavern door, he opened it and reached into his pocket and took out all of his remaining money. He tossed it on the floor of the tavern and said, "Chris has to live too," and weaved his way home.

Without question, Vic Palomaki's place was where most excitement happened and most stories were heard, especially on payday in the mines, Saturday night and during any celebration. His most loyal customers were found among the miners and the lumberjacks.

Vic was not one to get overly excited over anything. One of the more popular stories involved two women who were in a fierce fight—clawing, scratching and tearing at each other's hair. As they battled, they finally fell on the floor where the fight continued. Like all Saturday nights, the bar was full. Vic had all he could do to keep the beer tap open and fill the long line of empty glasses.

After Vic decided that the fight had gone on long enough, he turned to an old lumberjack sitting at the bar and said, "take a glass of this cold beer and splash it up their ass, and it will stop the fight." The lumberjack, feeling no pain, and well on his way to maximum consumption, took the glass and went behind the two combatants. As they rolled and struggled, their skirts were up over their backs, exposing everything and making a perfect target to follow Vic's instructions. When he came close, he bent over, he took careful aim and swoosh, the cold beer hit the intended sweaty targets. This resulted in the expected screams from the shock caused by the cold beer. Whatever fight might have remained in the two women ended abruptly.

Among clothing apparel, the most popular with the old miner and lumberjack were their caps. One was the woolen "Scotch cap," possibly named because of the red-or black-and-white checkered material from which they were made. These caps had rigid brims with ear flaps that could be folded on the inside or outside of the caps. In cold weather, the flaps were brought down over the ears to keep them from freezing.

The second cap was their famous fur hat brought from their homeland. These were sometimes referred to as "Cossack hats". They were often expensive hats made of the fur of beaver, mink, and other fur-bearing animals. Unlike the Scotch cap, the brim on the fur hat was kept up like the earflaps until needed. It didn't make any difference which cap many of the men wore when they were drinking. The more they drank, the brims began to act like a weather vane indicating the direction of the wind. At the beginning, the brims would be in the normal position over the forehead. As they got more involved and serious in their drinking, the brim on the fur hat would somehow come down and, like the rigid brim of the Scotch cap, begin to move to the side of the head. It would continue moving around the side of the head until it had turned a half-circle from its normal position. When the brim was turned the 180 degrees, it was a good indication that the man felt good, even though the limit of consumption was near.

Vic also served as a pawnbroker for many of his customers, especially the lumberjacks. Vic, like all bar owners of the time, was ready to lend money to his patrons. Though some alleged that it was against the law to sell drinks on credit, it was a problem easily resolved. No law restricted the barkeeper or bartender from loaning a friend a few dollars. If that friend chose to buy liquor with it, it was his business and not the state's to decide how it should be spent.

The lumberjacks usually decided that they wanted to leave their pocket watch as collateral until they returned from camp for the next drunk and to reclaim their watch by repaying Vic the money borrowed. I guess they thought their watch was useless while they were drinking. They would know when the bar closed by the lights being turned off. Sleeping in the city jail to sober off didn't require any timepiece. Waking up Sunday morning was the signal to go back to Vic's for an eye-opener. Even on their return back to camp located in the woods, didn't require a watch, as work was daylight to dark every day. Their watch, in reality, was an item to be used, only in keeping a record of any debt that was outstanding. If he had his watch, even for an hour or two, he knew that he was not in debt to Vic for that brief period.

Vic was very much like many of his patrons, a man who liked to tease and joke. On Sunday mornings, Vic would come to the tavern to clean up and get ready for reopening at twelve noon. As sure as day follows night, the lumberjack would leave the jail and go straight to Vic's only a block away. One morning while he was busy mopping up the floor, a lumberjack came in and sat down at the bar. After watching Vic going about his cleaning for a few minutes, he asked Vic what was good for the bad hangover he was suffering. With a straight face, Vic told him, "Water is the best thing for a hangover." Not impressed with Vic's answer, the lumberjack said, "The best is too good for a confirmed drunk like me. Just give me anything from one of the bottles behind the bar and that will be good enough." Vic smiled and went behind the bar. He reached for a bottle of whiskey and gave it to the man. Vic knew that the drink would be on the house because he had gotten the man's watch only a few hours earlier.

One story told often involved a Swede lumberjack working at a camp many miles from town. During a severe snowstorm, the logger went to the men's bunkhouse. He told them that it looked as though all operations would stop until the storm ended and the roads packed down again. Any of the men who wanted to go into town for a few days were told to go and return after the storm ended.

Ollie decided that he wanted to go into town and visit his girlfriend Olga. He packed what he needed in his packsack and went to a shed to get his traveling skis. Like all travel skis, his were homemade, coated with pine tar and ten feet long with both ends turned up. Putting his skis on, with packsack on his back, he started the many miles to his girlfriend's house.

Four days later, Ollie returned to camp in time for supper. After they ate, the lumberjacks gathered in the bunkhouse to discuss the events of the past few days. Someone asked Ollie what was the first thing he did when he got to his girlfriend's house. Ollie thought for a moment and said, "I yumped on Olga." Yeh, yeh, we know that would be one of the first things a horny bugger like you would do. What did you do after you had jumped Olga? Ollie went deep into thought and finally said, "Den, I take my skis off, and after tat I take off my packsack."

In their stories, dreams were involved, like in Himaka's dream about heaven and the mining company. Jim Blee, the same night watchman at the Athens Mine, and his lifelong buddy Mike Matighe were sitting in Tony's Bar when Jim told Mike of the dream he had the night before. In his dream Jim told Mike that both of them died at the same time. As they arrived at the pearly gates, St. Peter had the gates opened and welcomed both of them into Heaven. St. Peter looked at Jim and told him that Mike had been twice as good as he had been down

28

below. Because of this, Jim would be given only three wishes, which would be granted. Mike on the other hand would receive double of whatever Jim's wishes were.

When asked for his first wish, Jim asked for a hotel with one hundred nice rooms. Fine, no problem, said St. Peter. Mike will have a hotel with 200 nice rooms. "What is your second wish," asked the Saint. Jim responded by asking that a beautiful woman be put into each room, alternating between redheads, blondes and brunettes. "So it will be," said St. Peter, "and Mike shall have two of the same kind of beautiful ladies in each room of his hotel."

With only one wish remaining, Jim was so advised and told to be careful and sure of what he wanted in this last wish. Without hesitation, Jim looked St. Peter in the eyes and asked that one of his testicles be removed. Suddenly, Mike's double reward in heaven took a severe turn for the worse in Jim's dream.

There were two of our neighbors on Ann Street that provided many tall tales and came out with many statements that were remembered for a long time. Some were actual experiences but mostly stories that could well win awards in some liar's club contest.

Huck, Muck, and Other Characters

"Huck" Suline was another big man with unbelievable strength and equally unbelievable tales. He was a well-liked man, very good neighbor and one who loved children. Unfortunately, Huck and his wife never had children of their own, although he would have made a good father. Absent of kids of his own, he worshipped his nephew who lived only a block away.

Like clockwork, we could expect Huck to be at our house very early Christmas morning. Seeing the house lights on, he knew that my daughter and son were up and looking over the presents Santa had brought. On Christmas Day it was his custom to wear a woolen navy blue turtleneck sweater and big black tam, much like the one worn by artists. A gallon jug of wine would be carried in one hand and would be served in each of the houses he visited until it was gone.

Most all of his stories dealt with strength and power. One of the earlier stories was about his life growing up in Ewen where the Suline family once lived. In this small community, farming and logging were the primary occupations. For the 1893 Chicago World's Fair, lumbermen from the nearby community of Ewen displayed a sleigh piled high with 35,000 board feet of huge pine logs that had actually been pulled by a team of horses. Until recently, visitors to Ewen could visit a recreated exhibit of such logs at the town park.

Huck told of a time when a side or feeder track went off the main line to a loading area where logs were being sawed. A flat car that was loaded with the freshly sawed logs proved to be too heavy for the switch engine to move. Rather than remove any of the loaded logs, a local farmer was asked to bring in his big team of draft horses. Huck said the horses were big ones by anyone's measure, weighing a combined seven tons.

The team was backed up between the two tracks and hooked onto the flat car by heavy chains. The big horses lay almost flat on their stomachs as they strained to move the load. Finally the car began to move, but only after the horses had pulled so hard that the railroad ties turned around and broke the track spikes that held the iron rails. With every step of the horses on the way to the main line, the ties kept turning under the rails. I am no expert on the weight of horses, but I have never heard of any two horses that weighed seven tons. If there were such horses, one has to wonder how both could fit side by side between two regular railroad tracks.

In the same area of Ewen, according to Huck, was a man called Ollie who lived alone in a camp about seven miles from town. No one ever really knew the strength of this hermit and they decided to try and find out just how strong he was.

In his last trip into town before winter, Ollie came to pick up the staple foods for the long winter. These would include items like coffee, flour, sugar, salt, pepper, and such needs that couldn't be found in the woods. The woods provided other needs like venison, rabbit, partridge and wild berries.

Ollie first went to the local grocery store that also sold non-food items. While in the store, the owner asked Ollie if he could lift a hogshead filled with salt pork. The combined weight of the big wooden barrel and meat was over 500 pounds. If he could lift the barrel off the floor, the grocer promised him five dollars. "Hell, for that money I'd carry it home," replied Ollie.

The grocer laughed and told him that if he carried the barrel of pork all the way home, he could keep it and still get the five dollars. According to Huck, Ollie agreed to pick it up after he purchased all of his food order and picked up his mail from the post office.

When the time came for Ollie to return home, he went to the store. Ollie picked up his fully loaded pack sack and adjusted it over his shoulder. With the pack on his back and his mail in his pocket, Ollie turned the heavy hogshead on its side and, grabbing it from both ends, slowly balanced the barrel on top of the packsack. By wiggling and shifting the barrel, the weight was balanced to Ollie's satisfaction. As he left, he turned to the store owner and others who had come to watch, said goodbye and wished them well until he came to town again in the spring.

As Ollie walked away, the owner began to have doubts as to whether he might have to pay the bet. He sent his young clerk out to follow Ollie all the way home without Ollie's knowledge. After anxiously waiting for hours, the boy came back to the store. His boss wanted to know right away when Ollie had set the barrel down, which would mean that he would not have to lose the pork, plus the five dollars. The boy said he didn't know. He had given up following Ollie before he reached his cabin because he got tired of watching him pick blueberries with the barrel still on his back.

Still another of Huck's tales was of a Negaunee man who had a hunting camp north of the Dead River. This man had bought a medium-size Monarch kitchen stove. It was only a two-lid stove with a small oven, weighing about 250 pounds. The man had made a sling out of heavy hemp rope to carry the stove the three miles between the road and camp. After work on Friday, the man packed the stove into the trailer and had his wife drive him to the point where the trail led to his camp. By the time they reached this destination it was quite dark, but the man was sure that he could easily find his camp. He lifted the stove on his back and reminded his wife to be sure to come back late Sunday afternoon to pick him up.

His wife did return as scheduled, only to find that her husband hadn't yet come. She sat to await his arrival. As the time went by and darkness fell, she became worried and returned home to ask friends and neighbors to begin a search. An all-night search continued into Monday, with no luck. Finally, late Monday afternoon, Huck said, word came that the man had found his way out of the woods. Not anywhere near Negaunee, but in Iron Mountain, some eighty miles from his camp, still carrying the stove that he had put on his back three days earlier.

The original pinochle diamond was located just opposite the house I lived in, on the north side of the street. This was a meeting place where men played cards and told their stories. During one of these sessions, one of the men mentioned a picture he had seen in one of the national picture magazines. The picture showed a man holding a large pocket watch in his mouth. The watch was apparently at least three inches in diameter.

Huck said, "Hell, that's nothing to the man I saw in Chicago." He said he watched as this man carefully put nine regulation-sized pool balls in his mouth. After getting all nine into his mouth, the man turned to a pool table and quickly spit all nine balls out of his mouth like rice.

Yes, men like big Huck told their exaggerated stories. Their value was not in reality, but contributed much to the humor and easing of life in conditions that were not always the most enjoyable.

I don't remember why he left his job at the mines, but it may have been in the mutual agreement between the company and Huck, that each could survive without the other. He went to work for the City of Negaunee where employees would benefit by hearing Huck's stories.

One day I worried over Huck when I saw him bleeding badly from a gash on top of his head. He was fairly drunk and talking to himself while the blood covered his head and clothes. Though he had no known enemies on Ann Street, he apparently got into some argument with "Puffy" Wertanen. No fighting resulted between the two men, but as Huck was going out of the porch, Puffy picked up a maple ski and hit Huck over the head. The blow came close to knocking him out. Somehow Huck was able to get to our garage where he was found. After pleading with him, he finally agreed to be taken to Doctor Mudge and have the cut taken care of. Huck was not one to look for a fight, but he never ran away from one. Any prudent man interested in his own survival would want Huck on his side in any fight.

Like the majority of men on Ann Street, Huck liked his beer and other drinks, and was known by all bar owners. He limited his drinking to only two occasions, to drink alone or with someone. Though he may have had a rough side to his language in the eyes of some people, he also had the ability to put on the ritz and speak in the finest of words and tone of voice.

"Fat" Ruona never forgot Huck's meeting two good-looking women in his tavern. This incident occurred during a holiday when the town of Negaunee had many visitors. Sitting next to the two women, Huck brought out his very best language and pleasantries. As he spoke like the most refined person, Fat was taking something out of the safe behind the bar. He had never before heard Huck use such nice language or even knew he had the ability to speak such nice words. After several minutes of conversation with the ladies using such words as, "Ma'am," and making flowery comments on their looks and how well they were dressed, one of the women

33

looked at him and said, "Charlie, don't you remember us?"

Seldom did anyone refer to Huck by his real name, which caused Huck to move his head back a little and get a better look at the women. Not remembering ever meeting either woman, Huck continued his high-class language and said, "I'm sorry, I don't believe I've ever met either of you before. I'm sure I would have remembered...."

Suddenly he stopped. His memory had returned. "Ah, f_ _ k," he said. "You're the two whores I met on Ludington Street last year."

Once Huck and his good friend "Mud" Airaudi had been drinking for hours. They decided they had enough, and started for home in Huck's red bullet, the name for his Chrysler Royal. As soon as they got into the car, Mud fell sound asleep. A couple of hours later, Mud woke up to the sounds of tires speeding over the highway and the dashboard of the Chrysler looking as though it was on fire. That year's Chrysler had a speedometer light that changed colors according to the speed of the car. It started as a bright green color and began to change to a yellow at about thirty-five miles per hour. Gradually the color changed to orange and when the car hit sixty miles an hour it was a reddish color. Any speed over sixty increased it to bright red, indicating a dangerous speed. Hearing the tires and seeing the red dashboard, Mud looked out the window and saw lights and the moon reflecting on the surface of water. Even though half asleep and feeling the effect of hours of drinking, Mud knew that there was no water in the mile between Iron and Ann streets which had been the original destination.

He asked Huck, "Where in the hell are we?"

Huck just laughed and advised Mud that while he was sleeping, he had driven to Escanaba, seventy-five miles from Negaunee, seeking a different kind of entertainment.

Less than three blocks east of Huck's home lived another man who provided a lot of laughs with some of his talk. He had a nickname that was not much different

34

than his Muck. Most people called him "Muck" that rather than his real name, Toivo Kalmi.

Muck worked at the Negaunee Mine as Huck did. Muck never left the mine for another job and stayed until retirement. In his own way, Muck often expressed his own feelings in a way that was unusual. He was capable at times to charm anyone out of drink or to use deception in getting some of "Chicken" Louie's private stock of moonshine. Some looked at Muck as being paranoid, or one who liked to bitch.

Never one to look forward to work, he had ways of avoiding it when he found it impossible to go underground. Living as he did on the second floor of the house on top of Maki's Hill, his wife had a good vantage point to check if her husband really went to the dry, especially from the front porch. As Muck went through the sand cut and over the stretch of land between the cut and mine shaft, he was always in sight. However, when he went down the bank to the shaft area, he was out of sight. Whenever he concluded that the mine would get along without him for that shift, Muck turned away from the steps leading to the dry and went through the shop area and timber field to Lincoln Street. From there it was a straight shot to Iron Street and to Swan's Bar.

He always carried his lunch in a paper wrapper instead of a lunch pail. It was the same lunch, whether he ate it on the fourteenth level or in a booth. It was the afternoon shift that he most hated and especially on Saturday. That was the shift that he often pretended to go to work.

While sitting at the bar in one of his favorite taverns, Muck struck up a conversation with the stranger sitting next to him. It didn't take long for Muck to discover that the man was a car salesman for one of the car dealers in the area. Ultimately, this led to Muck telling the salesman that he was in the market to buy a new car.

Rather than sitting at the bar, the salesman invited Muck to join him and have dinner in one of the restaurants down the street. Muck accepted, and both left to discuss the possible sale of a car in privacy at the restaurant. After placing their order, the anxious salesman spread out all of his papers and publications about his car. The food was brought and Muck began to eat while the salesman feverishly pursued his sales pitch. To him, the fact that the food was before him had no importance compared to his anticipated commission.

Completing his meal, Muck told the man that he was sold on his car and the only question was as to what color his wife wanted. The salesman quickly gave Muck two dollars to take the cab home and return with the color. This would give the salesman a chance to eat his meal and wait for Muck's return. With a color chart and the two dollars in his pocket, Muck left the salesman and headed for home. It was not by taxi, or without a quick stop-over in Swans. With the money he bought a six pack of beer and walked home. I don't know how long the salesman waited for Muck to come back. I do know that Muck never bought a car, any car, from anyone.

Not long after the beginning of World War II, a group of Ann Street men and kids sat under a shade tree in the corner of our yard. It was a beautiful warm summer day, and Muck was scheduled to work the afternoon shift. Word came that the Athens Mine would be shut down until repairs were made in the mine's skip pit. (It was not unusual for the retaining wall in the Athens skip pit to break down.) This meant a hasty repair of the wall and a cleanup of the spilled mud and ore. The Negaunee Mine just opposite of the Athens, seldom had any major breakdown that interfered with production.

It was this difference in the two mines that caused Muck to go into the middle of Ann Street and pretend to look for enemy planes up in the sky. "If them goddamn Jap bombers ever fly over Ann Street, I'm going to point at the Negaunee Mine and tell them to bomb that mine if they want to stop production," he said, "Why waste a bomb on the Athens, that mine is always shut down."

It didn't matter what he would bitch about when Muck wanted to complain and get attention. The best example perhaps was his complaining about the absence of foreskin on his penis. He felt he was denied one of man's best pleasures without the foreskin. Those who had, Muck felt, had immediate sexual sensation caused by the movement of the foreskin. According to Muck, he had no such luck, and it took considerable rubbing with sandpaper before he got any feeling at all.

In a con similar to the one used with the car salesman, Muck used deception to get his hands on half a gallon of "Chicken" Louie's moonshine. Chicken Louie was always open for customers. Under his bed he always kept moonshine in various size bottles, including two quart Mason jars. To get moonshine during the night, it took only a tapping on Louie's bedroom window to wake him up. The window would open and the customer would place his order. Louie would get it from under the bed and reach for his money when he handed the booze to the person outside.

One night, Louie answered the signal and a strange voice ordered a half-gallon of moonshine. Louie obliged and reached out with the bottle, expecting to be paid the two dollars. He didn't get anything but a "thank you" in a voice that was no longer a strange one. It was Muck who had altered his voice when he placed the order.

Early Monday morning Chicken Louie came up Ann Street, out of breath and practically on the run. As he passed, men asked him what was wrong.

"That son-of-a-bitch Muck, he put the bone to Louie and never paid for my moonshine," he said. "I'm going to see Arne Pynnonen (Chief of Police). He'll make Muck pay."

Fortunately, they convinced Louie not to go to the police station and report the sale of moonshine that turned sour. It was no secret to the Chief that Louie had a lucrative business in moonshine as he had, I'm sure, tasted it himself on occasion. To have Louie come into the station raising hell and demanding help in this matter could well have harmed the relationship between the Chief and Louie.

Recalling the Old-Timers

As time passed, I learned more and more about the men around me. The majority of workers came from throughout Marquette County. Some came from the Chatham and Eben area of Alger County. A lesser number from the Copper Country area.

My father became friends with many men he had worked with over the years. I remember the names of three from the Gwinn area. They were "Maggie" Magnuson, "Chippy" Juidici, and Maruke Dellangello.

Chippy was one of many of the Juidici family who worked in the area mines, with long records of work in both salaried and hourly jobs. Maggie had only one eye, he had lost the other in an accident. While working with Maggie, they had a slice with curve, and the men running the tugger could not see the breast. Whenever this happened, one man would go to the outside of the curve and using his miner's lamp, would signal his partner. In this manner, he directed the operation and movement of the scraper. My father never forgot the day Maggie removed his glass eye and held it in his hand. He told my father to take the glass eye to the curve and he could run the tugger without my father's signaling.

Maruke, a stocky Italian, had lived most of his life in the Gwinn area before moving to Negaunee where his family lived on the county road. He told my father about the time he fed moonshine mash to a pig. The mash got the pig drunk and it ran through the fencing around the pen. Only after running throughout the neighborhood, were they able to catch the drunken pig and return it to the pen.

One summer weekend, my father went to help Maruke on some project. They completed the work just before noon on Sunday, and Maruke insisted my father stay for dinner. Like most Italian families, Mrs. Dellangello had prepared the fine and special food so popular for Sunday dinners. The food was spicier and hotter than my father was used to eating. He was always a man who enjoyed potatoes and gravy. But the last thing he would do was refuse the excellent meal and insult

38

Maruke or his wife! With almost every mouthful, he took a drink of Maruke's best wine served with the meal. He was no virgin to alcohol, but wine was not his favorite drink. It didn't take long before the wine took its effect. As soon as he took food from his plate, Maruke was there with more.

"He was good, eh Eino, eat more," he said to my father.

As the food kept coming on the plate, so too was the good wine refilling the glass. My father was in no shape after dinner to be of any help to his friend. Fortunately, their work had been done.

Bill Hakkola, a friend from Republic, had a deep voice and could be easily heard. Working on the midnight shift during a hot summer week, Bill complained about his neighbor's dog constantly barking, making sleep impossible. After a couple of days without sleep, Bill came into the dry and told the men that he finally had solved his problem. He said his neighbor's dog was a friendly son-of-a-bitch, and would come to him when he called. That morning he called the dog, rolled it over on his back and scratched his belly. As he was doing so, he picked up a cinder from the street. Bill slowly pulled back the dog's foreskin, put the cinder inside, then pulled the foreskin back into place over the cinder. For the rest of the day, Bill proudly boasted that the dog did not bark because it "was too busy licking its prick trying to remove the cinder."

Dogs were popular among the miners for hunting rabbits, watchdogs or pets. A good rabbit hound was worth its weight in gold for the avid hunter. Men boasted of their dog's speed, driving rabbits, obedience, and anything else.

One miner said the best hound could be identified in two ways. First, check its mouth to see if it had any teeth. If not, it met one test. A perfect hound was always right behind the rabbits. Without teeth, it could continue the chase without getting choked up by the hair of the rabbit as his mouth kept biting the rabbit's ass. The second measure was to check the direction the dogs prick pointed. If it pointed to the rear instead of the front end of the dog, you had the perfect hound. Facing to the rear protected the prick from getting caught on a log or brush as it chased the rabbit.

For many families, rabbits provided meat and it was prepared in many ways, all good. One of my favorite recipes was cooked by "Porky" Airaudi at the hunting camp. He used a lot of onions and various spices, then added wine and whiskey. This, with his polenta, was one of the favorites. Others cooked the rabbits in gravy, which was also a favorite of many.

Shotgun shells were not easily affordable with the low wages, and were totally out of reach during times when the mine was shut down. During these times, wild game provided most of the family meals. In the absence of shells, picture wire was made into snares. With snow on the ground, the rabbits' runways showed the route they took. Snares placed in these paths brought many of the rabbits to the table.

Some families raised chickens for eggs and meat. In a few homes, prize chickens were raised and kept more for show and pets. One man who had many varieties of prize chickens, was always caring for and pampering the birds. He was known to boast to others how he had the best breeds of chicken. There came a time when he began to notice a gradual decline in the number of his chickens. With strong suspicion but no proof, he believed that his neighbor was the chicken thief. He came up with a plan that he believed to be foolproof and would put a stop to the stealing. He searched around the area until he found a big police dog from one of the farms north of Negaunee. He bought the dog. Every night he would turn it loose to walk around the yard, knowing that it would bark and chase away any intruders.

With this security system in place, he let it be known to the suspected thief that no more chickens would disappear with the big watchdog patrolling his yard. It was not long after that at least six of his biggest chickens were missing. This bothered him to no end. He finally got the courage to confront his neighbor, the primary suspect.

He told the neighbor about his suspicions from the first time he knew that someone was stealing his chickens. At this point, he was so confident of the neighbor's thievery that he asked just how in the hell he got past the police dog. This was important to him, more important than the chickens that were taken the night before.

The neighbor laughed and told him that because of the man's bragging and boasting, he found a quick and easy solution. The neighbor also sought a dog, a female dog in heat. Then he waited until the man with the chickens went to bed and the watchdog was turned loose into the yard. The bitch in heat was put over the fence, and the last thing on the watchdog's mind was chickens. The neighbor said that the dog was so busy mounting the bitch that all he had to do was enter the chicken coop and pick the chickens off the roost.

The manager of Ann Street's softball team lived in a small room on the west end of a long chicken barn on Queen Mine Road. Old man Major, a bachelor, built himself a ladder wider than regular ladders, with the rungs on crosspieces farther apart. He leaned it on the west wall of the chicken barn. Major's outhouse was ready, with maximum room for all his needs. Without walls, the old man was often seen with his pants down, sitting on one of the crosspieces. In time, the pile under him became too high, but it didn't take any hard work such as digging a hole. All Major had to do was move up another rung to get more clearance.

Chapter 3—School Years

My formal education spanned the thirteen years from kindergarten through the twelfth grade in Negaunee Public Schools. As a five-year-old, my first day of school was in September of 1930. I graduated thirteen years later on June 13, 1943. Nowhere in the school records will one find any mention of academic awards or excellence.

Walking to School and What We Passed

The Park Street School was approximately a mile from home. The only way to get there was by walking. At no time during all of my school years was bus transportation provided for the students on the upper end of Ann Street, which resulted in all of us walking to and from school.

One way to get to the Park Street School was a short cut through the Negaunee Mine property. The longer route was to go along Ann Street, Healy Avenue and Case Street. The shortest path was the most interesting, but one where shoes and clothes got covered with iron ore. Though I had lived all my life on the south side of the Negaunee Mine shaft and stockpile, I had never before seen what was on the north side of the mine until taking this route.

Running west of the shaft was a long high trestle where tram cars would carry the rock and iron ore to be stockpiled. The waste rock was taken to the far end, the ore between the rock and the shaft. A natural passage was formed under the trestle where the rock and ore met. This was the opening we walked through to get to the north side. Here, we could see the mine shops and timber yard. In the yard were large piles of big timbers, cedar lagging, poles, planks and railroad ties. Trucks would be unloading more timber, and we could see the timber gang preparing and loading supplies for the miners underground.

On the western end of the mine property was the mine dump. Broken timbers and other combustible items from underground were burned at this site. Damaged equipment and machinery were set aside and sold to scrap dealers.

Bordering the timber yard was the access road to the Negaunee Mine office and dry house. Just inside the entrance stood a medium-sized brick building with a large vegetable garden. Both were inside a fence to protect against intruders. Later in life I learned that this building was used to store the vegetables from the garden.

In late winter, a crew of men would go to Negaunee's Teal Lake and cut large blocks of ice which would be brought into this building. There, it would be covered with sawdust from the timber field and carpenter shop. This would insulate the ice and keep it from melting for use in the summer. All the vegetables and the ice were for the mine superintendent and his family.

Near the brick building on city property was a larger building, the city fire station. Fire fighting equipment stored there was for use by the firemen. This building also served as the official voting place for Fifth Ward voters. At one time, voters had to declare their party of choice before receiving a ballot. In local elections, the choice had to be made between the People's Party or the Taxpayer Party. In state and national elections, choice was between the Democrat and Republican parties. Standing inside the voting station would be a salaried clerk from the mine, keeping a record of those miners selecting the People's Party and Democratic Party ballots. Obviously, they were not the favored parties of the mine officials.

The entrance to the mine property was an extension of Lincoln Street, where it intersected with Mitchell Avenue. At this corner stood a very large white house, so big that its back entrance faced Lincoln Street and the front faced Main Street, the next street to the north. This mansion-like home had a well-kept lawn and beautiful flowers. Surrounding the lot was a wrought-iron fence and large evergreen trees. To a kid of my age, it was not a house, the fence, lawn or flowers that made a big impression, but the large concrete swimming pool on the southeast corner of the lot. To kids who swam nude in water-filled mine pits, we could care less of wealth, power or prestige of a family so lucky to have such a nice home. It was only that swimming pool that we admired. This property was owned by a well-known family with holdings and interest in iron ore mining. It was the Maas family from which the Maas Mine got its name.

Directly opposite the Maas home on Main Street was another large house, not as admired as the Maas house as it had no swimming pool. Here lived the Negaunee Mine superintendent who had the exclusive use of the brick building and its contents at the mine entrance.

Looking down Main Street toward town from these houses was to us the most scenic of any street anywhere. Cement curbing and sidewalks ran on both sides of the street. Between curb and sidewalks stood big maple trees. Their branches met over the middle of the street, creating a tunnel-like effect to shade the entire width of the street. With the change of seasons, this cover of leaves changed from the green of summer to the bright orange and red of fall.

Just a couple of blocks from Main Street stood the Park Street School. Here on the corner of Mitchell Avenue and Park was my school for the first six grades.

By taking the shortcut, teachers could identify us as Ann Street kids apart from students of other locations. It was our ore-covered shoes that gave us away and led to special instructions to clean our shoes before entering the school. Other than that, we were treated like all other boys and girls, with no sign of prejudice.

Along Park and Mitchell was a family store owned by the Dighera family. On the west side was the Finnish Immanuel Lutheran Church. The store was a favorite place during recess. One could easily go there to buy and, if one had at least a penny. That would buy one of the many varieties that were in the showcase. It never became a routine or daily event, but an exception limited to that day when one had a penny.

The alternate way to school was much cleaner but less interesting than the short cut through the mine. We

44

could walk along Ann Street to Healy Avenue and to school. Healy Avenue had a store owned by Milton Lindberg with a large selection of nickel chocolate bars and penny candy. A double-dip ice cream cone could be had for a nickel. Anyone who ever watched a young kid with a penny looking over a big selection of candy knows that they take about as long to decide as an older person takes in buying a car. Yet the storekeepers always had the patience to wait for that important decision as to which candy would ultimately be chosen.

Life at School

At school, we were required to bring a spoon at the beginning of every school year. The teacher would write our names on a piece of tape and wrap it on the spoon. Every morning we would stand in line with spoon in hand. At the head of the line stood our teacher with a bottle in her hand. As we reached her, she would pour a thick brownish and terrible smelling liquid in our spoons. Every drop, including licking the spoon clean, had to be taken before moving away. Never before or since that time sixty years ago have I tasted a more terrible or worse smelling liquid than that daily dose of cod liver oil, a source of Vitamin D.

The second and equally unforgettable experience at the Park Street School involved the boy's lavatory. While in the fourth or fifth grade, my classmate Bob Leaf and I decided on a contest that involved the urinal. The test was not to stand in the front of the urinal to determine the winner, but to stand next to it and up close to the wall. The champion would be the one who would reach the highest point on the wall. What happened shortly after proved that we were both losers.

Somehow our principal, Maude Dawe, learned of our contest, and we were taken by the ear back to the lavatory. Pointing to the still-wet evidence on the plastered wall, she brought out a stiff wooden ruler. Ordering us to stretch out our arms and open our hands, she began handing out her punishment. Not to favor either side or either hand, she slapped both sides of each hand with vengeance. In retrospect, I suppose she could have chosen a different and more sensitive part of our body, and one more closely identified with the actual crime.

After leaving Park Street School, I went to the brand new junior high Central Grade School. Here, along with the kids from other elementary schools, were larger classes and new friends. Instead of the old short cut, we walked along the back road that extended west of Ann Street. This would bring us between the city fire hall, Honkavaara's Garage and Pioneer Avenue. Two blocks further was the Manual Training Building and next to it, the new school. I remember how much nicer and warmer it was than the old wooden Park Street School.

Memories of my years in junior high seem to blend in with the high school years. Wedged between the two came a two-week confirmation school. This began immediately after the end of the school year in June. My confirmation classes were at the Finnish Immanuel Lutheran Church. The minister at the time was new to this church and more stern and conservative than most others.

During one morning recess period, two of my classmates and I went to the Queen Mine cave-in, Ann Street's swimming hole. The water in this deep pit was usually cold on the hottest summer days, but in early June, it was even colder. We had a seven-shot water pistol with us that held at least a cup of water. This pistol could be emptied with one shot by pushing the lever all the way down. Filling the pistol to capacity, we went back to the church and school. Our plans were to shoot the girl in front of us in the first pew. Getting to church, we were confronted by the minister who gave us hell for being late before resuming his teaching.

Ironically, the topic was the Ten Commandments. As he preached against taking the Lord's name in vain, it looked like the right moment had come to use the water pistol. As my friends tugged at the gun to see which one would do the shooting, the lever was pushed all the way.

46

This resulted in all the water going on the crotch of one boy's trousers.

The shock of the cold water made him jump up from his seat and loudly say, "Jesus Christ, look what you did!"

What came after made the earlier tongue-lashing seem very minor. For the rest of that day's classes, our heads were bowed in prayer. Never before or since that day do I believe that anyone looked longer and more quiet as he sat looking only at his shoe tops and the floor. I don't know if Helvi ever realized that she was the intended target.

My first exposure to vocational training occurred in eighth grade at the Manual Training Building. There we had an opportunity to try our hand at woodworking, metal shop, machine shop and mechanical drawing. This primary training placed me in a better position to select which program I would take in high school. Each student had to select one of the three available programs: college preparatory, commercial, or vocational training in high school.

Teacher Condemnation

Choosing the vocational course was in the eyes and mind of one high school teacher "taking the easy way." For those of us from Ann Street, "the other side of the tracks," he went even further in his condemnation. We would become no-account drunk and dirty miners.

This experience burned into my memory and will never be forgotten, let alone forgiven. Content with his self-given, but misplaced prestige and power over students, this teacher stooped to the lowest level of man and attacked people he never knew, including our parents. He made non-relenting, blanket indictments of all underground miners who many years earlier had become my best role models. Miners, by the nature of their work, were dirty. Yes, many were heavy drinkers. Many others practiced temperance and church going. No account? Never! Any comparison between the miners and that judgmental teacher left no doubt in my mind as to who was the best neighbor and who contributed the most to society.

In his criticism of vocational courses, he in reality placed himself on a pedestal more superior than the teachers at the Manual Training Building. The reverse, however, was that teachers Mr. Vanni, Mr. T.C. Davis, Mr. Wilson, Mr. Daly and Mr. Hakenjos were head and shoulders above his level and far better teachers. I doubt whether any school has ever had better teachers in the area of vocational education than these five teachers.

This teacher, who was so critical of Ann Street people, proved in at least one instance that he was the more stupid. Found guilty of illegally shooting a doe, he was caught and paid the penalty. Reportedly, the deer was not killed for meat, but for the joy of killing. The violators of Ann Street, as most miners, illegally shot deer —not for pleasure but for food—but seldom got caught at it.

Teachers and Others

The school superintendent and principal were men of firmness and fairness. Every student recognized Superintendent H.S. Doolittle and R.G. Gillmore, the principal, when they came into the classroom or walked down the school halls or streets.

There were two others of equally strong discipline and fairness, the two MacCaullife sisters who taught school longer than most others. Neither sister ever married, and teaching was the most important part of their lives. Julia was a math teacher who used a unique way of creating interest in mathematics. Regularly, on Friday, she would have a contest to see who could give the quickest and most correct answers to the problems she wrote on the blackboard. The winner was given a dime at the close of the class.

This teacher also taught us a fast way of multiplying by the number eleven and to multiply any two-digit number ending in five by itself. Many years after leaving the Army, I bought a book on a new method of mathematics. I don't remember the title or spelling of

the man who developed this new and faster method—
something like Trachenberg. This Norwegian developed
it during World War II while a prisoner of the Germans.
Using whatever scraps of paper he could, he finally came
up with this new method. In the fifty or more years since
learning this way of mathematics, I have mentioned it to
college students. They in turn brought it to the attention
of their professors who apparently never heard of it.

The second sister, Nellie, was in charge of the
study period and the assembly hall. Sitting at her desk on
a raised platform in front of the hall, she had an uncanny
and unbelievable way of seeing whatever was going on
anywhere in the large hall. Appearing as though she was
reading or writing, she deceived us, often resulting in our
staying after school or extra homework. Like the modern
Stealth bombers, she would disappear from her desk and
go out into the hall, then reappear out of nowhere at the
back of the room. She would go from desk to desk of
those students caught exchanging papers, talking to each
other, or shooting spitballs, telling the guilty what their
punishment would be.

In woodworking classes, I learned how to properly
hold the handle of a hammer. One question in a test given
by Mr. Vanni dealt with this subject. A choice of three
answers was given: halfway up on the handle, one-fourth
way up, or at the end. Using my grip as the right way, I
answered one-quarter up on the handle. Seeing my
answer, Mr. Vanni came to my workbench and asked,
"Ernie, why do you think the handle is as long as it is, if
you aren't supposed to hold it at the end?" Years later,
whenever I hold a hammer, I think of Mr. Vanni and his
words.

Memories

My formal schooling came to an end on June 13,
1943, when I received my graduation diploma. The
longest memories of the thirteen years at the Park Street
School, Central Grade and high school with its vocational
training can be summed up as follows:

1. Never again take that vile-tasting cod liver oil.
2. Never get into a pissing contest with anyone, anywhere.
3. Never hold a hammer except at the end of the handle.
4. Never take a water pistol to church.
5. Never, never discriminate or hold prejudice against any man, woman or child because of their association with any group.
6. Always remember the teaching methods and dedication to her pupils as demonstrated by Julia McCaullife.
7. Remember the discipline and fairness of Mr. Doolittle, Mr. Gillmore, Julia and Nellie McCaullife, and Maude Dawe.

The Kids of Ann Street at Play

Every kid, especially boys, had regular duties they had to do. We helped with the wood, kept the wood boxes in the house filled, shoveled snow off the paths in the winter and did other chores. But we found time to play.

During the winter months we played basketball whenever someone had a ball. Our basket was a regular bushel basket with the bottom cut out and nailed to Cleven's barn. The basketball was not one made of rubber to keep it from getting wet, but made of leather. Some of the older models had lacings on them with a rubber bladder inside the leather cover. Regardless of which one was used, they got wet, heavy and deformed, more like the shape of an egg and the weight of a shot put than a basketball. The game was not like the game of today.

As small kids we often looked for empty evaporated milk cans. Hopefully, the cans would have only a small hole in them. We would lay the can down on the ground and pound the heels of our shoe or boot between the ends. This would crush the can down until the top ends would curl inward and tightly clamp onto our heels. With a can on each foot, we walked around like women on high heel shoes. After one use, they were no longer of any value except to one with narrower heels.

"Shacking cars," another game, was one of more danger, and in hindsight, very stupid. We would hide behind a snow bank at a street intersection waiting for a car to come to a stop. After the car stopped, we would sneak behind the car and grab the rear bumper that extended behind the body and rear fenders. Like a skier, we would crouch down and slide on our shoe bottoms down the street while tightly hanging on. Any unexpected bare spot on the street would cause a serious fall. A sudden braking of the car did little good for the teeth, mouth or nose. There were hundreds of homemade mittens lost due to this game of "shacking cars." Wet or damp woolen mitts stuck hard to the cold steel bumper. Even though the hand left the bumper, the mitten kept going.

Riding High

Ski riding began on small hills built in the yard. As time went by, larger hills were used. Skis varied from homemade barrel stave skis to store-bought. Riding down the sand cut on barrel staves was a challenge. If you didn't clear the railroad tracks between the snow banks, a nasty fall was the result. Ski hills and bumps were made on Little Hill and a hill behind the Athens Mine dry. Perhaps the most foolish attempt to ride skis was our attempt to ride down slopes such as the Athens Mine rock pile, preferably out of sight of our parents. Those familiar with the stockpiles know that in addition to being as high as the trestle, there was the steep angle of the pile to the ground, then another sharp angle where the two met. To get to the top of the pile you had to crawl and push your skis ahead of you. Because the wind usually blew most of the snow off the pile, there was very little snow on the top. Once at the top, one wondered why anyone would make such an effort to get there, especially as they began to fear what could happen on the way down. I don't believe that anyone ever rode the stockpile without taking a spill when they reached bottom. Few returned for a second try.

Sleigh riding down Alongo's Hill was one of the most popular winter sports. With a good sleigh, we could ride this long hill with its sweeping curve as far as the Queen Mine. To avoid running into an oncoming car, we sent someone to the end of the run to signal the driver to stop if someone was coming down the hill. Riding down the hill with its long ride was much more enjoyable than climbing back to the top. It was told that a visitor from China who had taken his first ride down a toboggan run was asked what he thought of the ride. His answer was "Zip—walk back up hill for one mile."

We also rode on big pieces of cardboard or toboggans. A piece of old galvanized sheet iron often served as a toboggan. By bending it up on one end, it formed a curved front. It only needed a hole in the front to tie a rope or wire for pulling it back up the hill. Previously used sheet iron always had jagged holes where nails had been used. This thin sheet with its corrugated face and nail holes didn't make sitting comfortable, nor did it do our clothes any good as they were ripped and torn by the jagged steel.

Summer Activities

During the summer we played softball, swam in the swimming hole and learned how to shoot a .22 rifle. Softball was limited to playing either in the narrow avenue or equally-narrow strip of land between the sand cut and the Negaunee Mine. In either place the odds were high that someone would hit the ball into a yard, or worse, break a window or hit the ball down the sand cut or incline to the mine. Like our basketball, a softball soon became deformed and heavy after getting wet and falling into the mud that was always present near the mine. A softball was not easy to replace. When the cover started to fray we would use friction tape to temporarily hold it together. After losing the cover, more tape was wrapped to keep the string from unraveling off the ball. With a loose cover, tape, or strings, when it was in the air, the ball looked more like a propeller than a ball.

Our swimming hole was the Queen Mine cave-in not far from the base of Alongo's Hill. This old mine cave-in was not the usual kind of swimming hole. There were two small bays on the north side and an old rock pile on the opposite bank. The water was a dark green color, possibly leeching from the rock pile or old mine workings. The bottom was covered with sharp slate-like rocks instead of beach. To swim all the way to the rock pile and back qualified one as a swimmer. Almost every kid on Ann Street learned to swim and was watched by Hunno Mattson, an excellent long-distance swimmer. He made sure that we were good enough to try to swim the hundred or so feet before letting us attempt it. Even then he would be close by and swimming alongside to help when necessary. One of the bays was solely for the Ann Street gang, the other for the kids living on Buffalo Hill.

One game was to throw a white object into the water and see who could find it. A white cosmetic bottle or white rock served the purpose.

A diving board made out of an old plank from the mine was used when we got brave enough to jump feet-first into the water. No one ever wore a bathing suit or trunks of any kind, so our left hand was used as a supporter by cupping the hand around the testicles to protect them from injury. It was a comical sight to see someone running toward the end of the board holding his crotch with the left hand and either holding his nose with the right hand or extending the arm high over his head and shouting, "Geronimo!" I never understood why we hollered "Geronimo" as we left the board, but perhaps it was our imitation of a paratrooper jumping out of a plane and shouting the name of that great Indian chief Geronimo.

One summer, four of us went camping at Champion Beach. As soon as our tent was pitched and the grownups returned home, we went for a swim. In the park everyone had to wear swim trunks, which we purposely bought for this trip. Not far from the shoreline there was a diving board and platform built on a raft. We swam straight to the raft and began to jump off the diving board. Even though we were wearing trunks with the built-in support, the force of habit made us grab our crotch with one hand and shout "Geronimo" as we left the diving board. This drew a lot of spectators on shore who undoubtedly wondered where in the hell we came from. As a matter of fact, Chick Koskela, the lifeguard, asked us this very question.

Target Practice

As soon as my father thought I was old enough to learn how to shoot and handle a .22 rifle, he took me to the city garbage dump. At that time the city dumped all of its garbage into an old mine pit. The pit was about a quarter mile south of the Athens Mine and near the Patch Location. In the evening, when city workers were not on duty and the dump truck stopped hauling, the dump came alive with hundreds of rats running among the garbage, seeking food. There was always a smoldering fire; the smoke was strong smelling and thick. Bottles could be heard exploding from the heat of fires. The rats were big and often crippled by being shot or by some other cause. Lying atop a small grassy mound, we didn't wait long for our moving targets. This dump provided many boys with the opportunity to learn about safe shooting and gun handling.

With the beginning of winter, the rats found easy refuge and food by coming to Ann Street houses and cow barns. They would return to the dump again in the spring, when hunting rats would start again.

"Playgrounds"

The old abandoned mines and cave-ins provided more dangerous playgrounds. In addition to our swimming hole in the Queen Mine cave-in, there were two other deep mine pits filled with water between Ann Street and the Buffalo Hill location. Forming a triangle with the Queen Mine, there were the Prince George and

Prince Edward Mine pits. I am not sure of these names, except that they were the names most often heard. Even after the Queen Mine ceased operations and the buildings were torn down, some of the bigger surface machines were left to rust on their concrete footings. One accident involving this old equipment left me with the little finger on my right hand deformed after I ripped it open in the gears of one machine.

Between the three pits and Ann Street stood the skeleton of the old Lucky Star Mine shaft. This shaft was all that remained of that mine and created a challenge to many boys to climb as high as they dared along the steel braces and beams. To one boy, the shaft proved not to be lucky. "Bull" Saari climbed the shaft with a large umbrella. The umbrella was to be his parachute and give him a safe and soft landing when he hit the ground. Rather than opening like a parachute, it opened up like a funnel, and both umbrella and Bull came down like a rock. Fortunately, Bull only suffered a fractured ankle — a lesson to others that an umbrella is no substitute for a parachute and that no mine shaft was ever designed for boys to climb and jump from.

The water, pumped out of the Athens and Negaunee Mines, ran into ditches that carried the water to the Carp River east of Ann Street. One of the ditches was called Orey Creek because of its ore color. A second creek was named for a family that owned the land where the creek ran.

Over the years, the Carp River provided a good spot to go fishing, with its many brook trout. Where the mine water flowed into the river, the water was the same dark red color as it came out of the mines. As the river flowed toward Lake Superior, it gradually changed back to its natural color. There were three special names given to the river within a mile of Negaunee. The first was Orey Creek, where the water was the reddest; then came Rocky Carp, so-named because of the slate rock along the bank; finally, Sandy Beach where kids could wade in shallow water with a sand bottom.

Men—Softball, Pinochle

The men of Ann Street also had their favorite games and interest in the outdoors. One of their favorite summertime sports was softball. Not the slow pitch game of today, but the original fastball game. One of the best and most watched teams was the Ann Street team sponsored by the Lee Brothers Beer Distributors of Negaunee. The three brothers distributed Rahr Beer, a product of a Green Bay brewery. Never has any team of any sport been as loyal and big consumer of their sponsor's product than the Lee Rahr Softball Team. The original team members all came from Ann Street. Among them were the four Mattson brothers, Cossack, Art, Bill and George; "Porky", "Mud" and "Gumballs" Airaudi; Fred Beauchaine; Suppine Saari; Gent Chetto; and Carl Danielson. The team mascot, "Smokey" Nocenti, lost his father in a mine accident. The team manager was Major Trip.

Dressed in green and white jerseys and caps, they played ball from early summer to late fall. They played against many good teams, including teams at the Marquette prison. Playing at the prison was to play one of a number of different teams within the walls. All prison teams were good teams, capable of playing against any outside team. As inmates, they had a lot of time to practice, and the state provided the best equipment. The inmates were friendly to the teams they played from outside the walls and appreciated the competition.

The Rahr team always left the prison with new softballs, bats and gloves. Somehow, with the aid of trustees, this equipment found its way into their equipment bag, even under the watchful eyes of the prison guards.

Major Tripp, the team manager, was a heavy man and spoke with an English accent. He was a man of great emotion and competitiveness. He often came to tears as he watched his team committing errors, especially their inability to hit the ball during the early innings of the game. These flaws in fielding and hitting were at their worst during the early morning tournament games, especially on weekends and the day after payday. With vision blurred from the previous night's activities, the players would have the choice of any one of a number of balls they saw coming. They could not be blamed if they picked out the wrong ball to catch or to hit.

As Major watched these futile attempts, tears would run down his cheeks. He could be heard muttering: "What's wrong with thay buoys, thay ain't 'ittin?" After a couple innings and with normal vision restored, the players could focus on only one ball at a time. Then they could hit and field the ball with the best. A smile would return to old Major's face and he would say, "Thay buoys are 'ittin now," and be confident of the outcome of the game.

Playing pinochle was another favorite pastime during nice weather. Opposite our house was a pinochle diamond where cards would be played whenever four players got together. Sitting cross-legged, they would play for hours.

An annual pinochle tournament was scheduled on one weekend in the fall. It was held at the Maple Grove on the lower end of Ann Street, named for the large maple shade trees. Kegs of beer were put in wash tubs and packed in ice to keep them cold. Early losers could be found sound asleep under the shade trees, resting for the next round of games. The women brought lunch to the players. The games would end with the coming of darkness, or until at least four players could no longer hold or clearly see the cards. The players would head for home on legs less steady, to wait another year for the next tournament. Bridge and smear were played indoors during the winter months and often included the wives.

Hunting Dogs

One of the most prized possessions of many men were their rabbit hounds. The dogs were a mixture of fox hound, beagle, bloodhound and whatever breed present at the time of conception. Many dogs were also house pets and favorites of the kids.

Late summer and early fall was a prime time to train the young hounds to drive rabbits. The men would take their dogs east of Negaunee to Muck Swamp, another landmark named after an early Negaunee family. There they would set the dogs on a fresh scent and begin to chase the rabbit. While the hounds chased their prey, the cards would come out and the game started. One would stop the play and tell the others, "Listen, my dog is in the lead," as a way of bragging that his hound was the best and fastest of the pack.

On one occasion, "Ham" Niskonen had his old reliable hound Moo-soo along. As they played cards, Ham frequently stopped and reminded the others which dog was leading the pack. Ham had a habit of beginning every statement with the words, "Hulleh hulleh." After stopping the game many times by telling the others, "Hulleh hulleh, listen, old Moo-soo is still in the lead." Finally Supine Saari asked Ham to look behind him. While Ham was bragging over his Moo-soo, the old dog lay sprawled out soundly sleeping behind him. Old Moo-soo was more interested in sleeping in the warm sunshine than running after a scared rabbit with a bunch of barking young pups.

It didn't take long for Ham to wake Moo-soo from his sound sleep to send him after the rabbit. Rudely awakened by his master, the old hound started to bark immediately, even though he was nowhere near either the rabbit or the other dogs.

Deer Hunting

I doubt if any of us ever forgot our first deer-hunting trip. My first trip included camping in a nine-by-twelve-foot tent with my father, my uncle Jack Renfors, Walfred Prusi and Fred Beauchaine. The tent was pitched on the weekend prior to the opening of season on November 15. For years before my first year of hunting, they had tented in the Big Bay area. This year our tent was pitched on the Hunter's Roost Road.

How could I forget those few days with these four men, who had been friends and hunting partners for so long, sleeping together and eating on a bed made out of poles and straw covered with an old carpet?

The bed, built across the entire width of the tent, took up one half of the space, leaving room for only a small oil drum stove and a table. Although I was only thirteen years old, my father had given my age as fourteen when he bought the hunting license, as fourteen-years-old was the legal age to hunt. At night, in the dim light of a kerosene lamp, I would watch and listen as these grown-up men talked of their childhood, the mines where all four men worked underground and of earlier hunting seasons.

Walfred and my father spent a lot of time together. I remember times when they returned from a trip into the woods with a load of wood in Walfred's pickup truck, the carcass of a deer concealed under the wood. It was the deer that they really went after. The wood was used to hide their kill.

On the way home from Big Bay, they would stop at the Airport Inn near the Negaunee airport. During these stops, they visited with the owner, John, as they drank beer. John was known to be a wheeler-dealer and one who got involved in many transactions, either buying or selling. When asked how things were going and what he was up to, John answered that things were never better. He was currently involved in lumber dealings. He said that he was buying lumber for eighteen dollars per thousand board feet and selling it for sixteen dollars. They said he must have made a mistake. He must be buying lumber for sixteen dollars and selling it for eighteen dollars, with a profit of two dollars. "No," said John. "You heard me right. I buy it on credit and sell it for cash, making a profit of sixteen dollars for every thousand feet sold."

Movies

Going to the movies at the Vista Theatre was always an adventure. Saturday movies were a dime and fifteen cents for weeknights and double features. Friday nights and Saturday matinees were the best. Friday was usually double feature night. With no school the next day, we could stay up later. Saturday afternoon always featured a film of interest to most kids, along with a long-running serial. Some serials ran for fifteen weeks, which made it critical to go every Saturday until the end of the serial.

Sometimes it was more interesting to watch the older boys and girls carrying on high up in the darkest part of the balcony. Mr. Rytkonen had an uncanny way of sneaking up on a hugging and kissing couple and ordering them to stop whatever they were doing.

Those of us too young for the balcony tried to anticipate love scenes with kissing or hugging. We would duck down on our knees and hide behind the back of the seats. The bravest among us would sneak a look and tell the rest when it was safe to come up after the mushy scene.

Normally we would go home along the back road behind the fire hall and the Furnace Location. After a scary movie, Lincoln Street seemed to be the safest way because of its streetlights. Even with the lights, we would still run between lights, fearing that monsters lurked in the dark shadows.

Family and Community Ties

These early years on Ann Street were the best and perhaps the most formative of my life. To have lived and associated with so many good people of all ages, from so many ethnic groups and varying faiths, was a privilege and honor not enjoyed by everyone.

These people, like all others, were not without fault. Disagreements did not damage their friendly relationships or last long. The friendships and ties between families, beginning with the first generation immigrant family, still continue and are as strong almost a century later.

Never did I have a sense of any bias or prejudice among them. They did not pretend to be anything but the friendly and hard-working people they were. They had a strong conviction and determination not to seek self-serving power, prestige or profit, but were strongly motivated to do their best to make the future a little better and brighter for those who followed them in future generations. Without doubt, in that effort they were successful. To them, we all owe a debt of gratitude and thanks for a job well done, very well done.

I am convinced that others who have had the same good fortune to have lived among other immigrant miners in other mining communities show the same respect and have the same fond memories as I have for the immigrant families of Ann Street.

The BB Gun

Somewhere between the ages of 10 and 12, I got my first BB gun for Christmas. It was a lever-action Daisy that came with a supply of BBs and targets. As soon as daybreak came, I put a target on the barn wall and began to shoot my new gun. As soon as the immediate novelty wore off, I took the target down to show friends as I went from house to house to see their presents. A few hours later I returned home to find a group of men lined up on the porch waiting their turns to shoot my new gun. In the group were my father, grandfather, Uncles Jack and Axel and a neighbor "Huck" Suline. Huck was the only non-hunter in the group. All others had been hunters since they were big enough to hold a gun and *only* after they had earned enough money to buy a shotgun or rifle.

A new target had been put up and, as these grownups were shooting, the safest spot on the wall was the target. One look at the erratic movements of the gun barrel was enough to see that each man saw more than the one lone target through the gun sight. In their eyes, at that hour on Christmas morning, the targets were not only moving but colored red, the color of their eyes. Not even by accident did they hit the only target on the wall, but the BBs bounced wildly off the wall all around it. While all of this target shooting was going on, a familiar blue car stopped by and everyone knew it's owner was Doctor William Mudge. The good doctor was returning from making a house call to one of his patients living on the lower end of Ann Street. Doctor Mudge came onto the porch to see what was going on and to wish everyone a Merry Christmas. This doctor was no stranger to those on the porch as he had treated them as miners working for the Cleveland Cliffs Iron Company and as their family doctor.

If there ever was a contrast between men this was it. The doctor was never a hunter or gun user. Neither was he a drinker or a user of tobacco. The other men were all skilled as drinkers and had used tobacco for most of their lives. If they didn't smoke the tobacco, they used snuff or chewed Peerless. Huck was like the doctor in one respect, as neither had ever owned a gun. Doctor Mudge got caught up in the excitement and activity and soon had his turn. In his hands the barrel of the gun was unlike the others. It was steady and it immediately became obvious that he saw only the one motionless target through the gun sight. The target was no longer the safest place on the wall as holes began to appear on it. Knowing that he was a busy man the others told him to shoot as long as he wanted. After a few more minutes of target shooting he turned the gun over to the others. As he was returning to his car, he walked his familiar fast way and with his usual smile waved back and again wished everyone a Merry Christmas.

Though it was Christmas Day, it was like any other day in Doctor Mudge's busy life. His patients' illnesses or injuries didn't take a holiday, and neither did he as long as they needed him. After he left, the others, in disbelief, or perhaps shocked at what they had seen, turned back to take their turns with the BB gun. Their renewed efforts proved just as futile as before as the BBs hit everything but the target.

Having watched everyone but me using the gun, I began to complain and to plead for my gun. Uncle Axel quickly responded by telling me, "Don't be a kid for all of your life," and the shooting continued, but not for long. Finally, the two cardboard tubes once filled with BBs were empty. There would be no more shooting that day as no store would be opened until the next day.

I don't know how long that BB gun lasted, but the memory of that Christmas morning will never fade from memory. What I learned in hindsight was that there were lots of kids on that porch. What I saw in the eyes of every man, including the doctor, were the smiles and eyes of excitement of every boy when they got their first BB gun. The gun they held and shot was the one they never got as young boys, but that morning for the first time in their lives that gun was theirs, if only for a short while. Why shouldn't they be just as excited and happy even if it came so many years later in their lives? All I had to do was wait for those ten or twelve years to get my BB gun and surely, in retrospect, I had nothing to complain about.

Jasper Street

Jasper Street in Ishpeming was a street very much like our Ann Street. We often visited relatives living on Jasper Street. One aunt and uncle lived in a white house surrounded with a wrought iron fence on the corner of Jasper and Marquette. Of my father's four sisters, my favorite was Aunt Tyni, who lived further east on the same street. Tyni and my father had a close attachment to each other, and both had a good sense of humor. A bus ran regular schedules between Negaunee and Ishpeming. We boarded at the stop at the Breitung Hotel, got off at Marquette Street in Ishpeming, and walked the short distance to Jasper Street.

During our Sunday visits we would enjoy the food prepared by Aunt Tyni, who was an excellent cook and baked some of the best bread and biscuits one could hope for. One of her specialties was angel food cake. She would make it whenever she had filled a quart mason jar with egg whites. Like so many of the older Finns, she wouldn't think of brewing coffee without an egg yolk and a little salt mixed in with the coffee grounds. The whites were put into the jar until it was full, and then came the angel food cake.

My father liked to tease Aunt Tyni. Regardless of how many times he saw a cake on the table, he would ask her what happened to her picture-perfect cake because it looked lopsided, or hadn't been baked right, or whatever possible complaint came into his mind. She would blame it on the weather conditions, chickens that laid the eggs, her oven or any other imagined problem.

Our relatives spoke of other immigrant families living on Jasper Street and other parts of Ishpeming. The Erkilla's, Pellonpaa's, Biettila's, Maki's, Hans Anderson and many others. The Jarvinen family had come to this country on the same boat as the Otto Ronn family; both families settled on Jasper Street. Frank Jarvinen, one of the sons, became my godfather. We lost touch with each other for a long time. On one of my later birthdays, Frank surprised us by coming over with a card and a gift of money. Frank had already been retired for some time, and I had mixed emotions over the ten dollars he had put inside the card. Knowing that he was on limited income and I was still working, I told him that his coming to visit was the best possible gift I could hope for and suggested that he take the money back. He would have no part of that. He said he wanted to do something for my birthday, and that he had not forgotten. Before leaving, Frank asked if we liked raspberries. He promised to bring us berries when they ripened.

The next day I took the birthday money to Muelle's Nursery in Marquette and bought a sturdy, well-developed crimson maple tree. I took the young seven-foot tree and painstakingly planted it in front of our house. This was to be my godfather tree, that would grow big and last for years. When Frank came with the raspberries, I showed him the godfather tree I had planted in his honor. The tree came through the winter in good shape and looked strong and growing. It was not long after Frank's last visit that he died. For some unknown reason, the godfather tree died shortly after.

As I grew older I heard more about life and some of the people of Ishpeming: stories about the Salisbury Location where moonshine of high quality was available; merchants like the Rosburgs, Loftburgs, and Lowensteins; professionals like Doctor Holmes, Doctor Erickson, Dentist Piirto and Attorney John Voelker. My father worked as a teamster for Mr. Rosburg and delivered groceries with horse and wagon. Doctor Piirto, I believe, was a classmate of my father during his eleven years of schooling.

John Voelker was a lifelong friend of my father and they apparently got into their share of mischief. After his surgery for cancer, my father lived with my family. One evening while reading the "60 Years Ago" feature in The Mining Journal, he smiled and laughed over the reference to the theft of a penny candy dispenser from the front of Lowenstein's store. The store owner posted a public notice claiming that the names of the two boys were known and that if the candy and dispenser was immediately returned, they would not be prosecuted. My father wondered out loud if perhaps two innocent boys may have been punished. The machine still rests at the bottom of one of Ishpeming's mine pits where it was thrown by John Voelker and my father, but only after it was emptied of the penny jaw breakers.

Chapter 4—Underground, Day One (June 21, 1943)

The month of June, 1943, was a turning-point in my life. In particular, the nine days between June 13 and June 21. During this period, I rode an emotional roller coaster.

On Sunday, June 13, my school days came to an end when I graduated from Negaunee High School. This was a day of joy and happiness that I had looked forward to for thirteen years. The next day was one of waiting for Tuesday, June 15, my eighteenth birthday. This was the day that I had to register for the military draft under the Selective Service Act. In that same day, I applied for a job with the Cleveland Cliffs Iron Company.

Preparation for Work

Early Tuesday morning I went to the Negaunee City Hall and to the office of City Clerk, Jake Anderson. After registering for the draft, I went straight to the Cleveland Cliffs employment office at the Brownstone in Ishpeming. "Brick" Sundberg interviewed me and had me fill out an application. After completing the application, I was told to report to the Ishpeming Hospital at 8:00 a.m. on Wednesday, June 16. Brick told me to return to this office on the morning of June 21 to get the results of my examination by Doctor Waldie, the company doctor. He said that I would be hired if I passed the exam.

The weekend was long and worrisome. Would I pass the physical? When and where would I work? Who would be the first to take me? Would President Franklin Roosevelt claim me for service in World War II, or would I go into the mine working for Cleveland Cliffs?

On Monday morning, I was at the employment office before it opened. Mr. Sundberg gave me the good news that I had passed my physical. He asked me if I had any preference as to which mine I would be assigned. I told him that I lived between the Athens and Negaunee Mines, and that my father and uncle worked at the

Negaunee Mine, as my grandfather had before his accident. He gave me a "Report for Work" slip to the Negaunee Mine and directed me to go to the mine immediately. I was walking on cloud nine.

The next stop was the Negaunee Mine office. From the supply room I was given a hard hat, lamp belt, rubber gloves and safety glasses. A clerk gave me my brass check number and scheduled me to report for the midnight shift on Monday, June 21, 1943.

As Monday ended, I was ready for work. I returned home to pick out clothes that would be suitable for wearing underground. These included an old flannel shirt, a suit of two-piece winter underwear and woolen socks. Other items had to be purchased. Mining boots, overall pants and jackets came from Levine's Department Store, a lunch pail from Perala Hardware. After everything had been gathered, I placed them into a burlap sack along with a towel, washcloth, and a bar of soap. Everything was nearly ready before going to bed; all that remained to do was to take my burlap bag to the mine and hang the mine clothes in the dirty clothes dry and take the empty sack, towel, washcloth, and soap to my assigned locker in the other dry. The rest of the day was spent anxiously waiting for nightfall and actually going to work on my father's shift.

At 10:30 p.m., my father took our lunch pails and we were on our way to the mine. As I walked along the well-worn path down the sand cut to the mine, I thought of the many times my father had walked this route since his first day of work some twenty-one years earlier. Like others, my uncle, grandfather, and so many neighbors had traveled this route for thirty years or more.

In the dark of night, the mine took on a different appearance. The long shadows cast by the lights on the trestle and landing were not there in the bright of day. Even the sounds and smells seemed different in the night air. One of the first changes I noticed as I entered the dry was that the long sink with its many wash basins had been removed. A shower room had replaced them. The miners now could shower and clean up before changing into their street clothes and returning home.

After dressing in mining clothes, I looked around the dry at other men. Some I recognized from the time I carried lunch pails to my father and grandfather, but they were much older now.

Working Underground

One new man in the dry was no stranger— he was a classmate of mine. We had ended our school days and were starting a new career together. Kenny Anderson and I were also scheduled to work together on this first shift underground. I picked up my miner's lamp and filled a half-gallon glass water jug. Nothing more had to be done except to wait to be checked in.

Shortly before 11:30 p.m., the night watchman came into the dry and unlocked the doors to the checkroom. Each man picked up his own brass check and the watchman recorded them on the time sheet. As the afternoon shift came up, they would toss their checks into a box and the watchman would check them out. Regular timekeepers checked the day shift in and out, along with checking in the afternoon shift. Jim Dompierre and Bucky Backlund were two of the regular checkers. Both seemed to know every miner's check number and automatically checked them in as they walked by.

As the contract miners left the checkroom, many picked up fuse cans that had been filled with capped fuses, ready to be used underground. They carried them over their shoulders, along with their water jugs.

As I passed the open door to the outside, I looked out into the warm June night, then took my first step down the long stairway that I had looked down so many times as a kid. I began counting—one, two, three... I didn't stop counting until I stepped off step fifty-two and into the long tunnel between the shaft collar, the timber yard and the shops. A long line of timber trucks was parked along the tunnel tracks and side tracks. Trucks loaded with a variety of supplies were ready to go underground. Others carried broken tools, equipment, and timbers that had been hauled out of the mine.

Coming around a curve in the tunnel, I stood before the iron gate at the collar of the shaft waiting for the cage to come to the surface. Soon the bell signals rang, indicating the cage was being loaded to bring afternoon workers to the surface. After both decks were loaded, the signal was given to the hoisting engineer to begin hoisting the cage. As I watched the steel cable slowly move, in my mind I questioned how such a small cable of steel could hoist the heavy cage and the forty men in it. The rope began to move faster and faster as it left the level below. Soon we heard the rattle of the cage doors and voices of the men talking. These sounds became louder and the cage rope gradually slowed as the cage came nearer to the landing. When the top of the cage moved past, I noticed how the steel cable was attached to the cage. The cable ran through a heavy steel eye and looped back and attached to the cable. There, the cage rope was held above the cage with a number of steel clamps and bolts. Later, I learned that these were called crosbys.

As contract miners came out of the cage, they would stop to tell their opposite partners which supplies were needed and about any problems waiting below. The cage was emptied. I stepped into the cage for the first time. After loading, the boss signaled the hoistman to lower the cage and to what level. Slowly the cage moved down the shaft and began to speed up. As the cage sped by the lower levels, only a brief second of dim light could be seen from the opening above the cage door. As the cage came near the level where it would stop, it progressively slowed until coming to a halt. The hoistman signaled that the cage was now stopped and it was safe for the men to get out.

Stepping out of the cage was like going into a strange new world. Like a kid in a toy store, I didn't know where to look first. The area was congested with both afternoon shift men ready to go home and men just coming on shift. Miners who hadn't seen their opposite partners on surface were now getting the same information regarding supplies and the condition of their workplace.

This large area next to the shaft was fairly well illuminated, especially on the plat where ore was dumped into the pockets. The plat, separated by a pillar of rock, was elevated enough to allow the motor crew chuteman and brakeman to dump the cars. A big chalkboard hung on the side of the plat where the motor crew recorded the number of ore cars and the contract from which it came. At the end of the shift, the bosses would tally and record the number of cars pulled from each contract.

Tracks were lined up even with the tracks on the bottom of each deck on the cage. As in the tunnel, trucks were standing near the shaft. Some were ready to return to the surface for loading, others were loaded and ready to be brought back into the mine.

Fifty-gallon oil drums mounted on stands were stationed in this area. Miners filled their oil cans with oil for their machines. Kegs full of six and eight-inch spikes were open. Miners took them as they passed.

Nearby, a big pump room that had been blasted out of solid rock housed the huge water pumps. Pumps constantly pumped hundreds of thousands of gallons of water out of the mine every hour.

When we got off the cage, the congestion ended as quickly as it had started. Only a few men remained in the area. The motor crew with the loaded train on the plat began dumping the ore. Other motor crews left the shaft area with their motor to hook up to the cars left inside. After most of the men started inside, these motors would slowly move along, ringing their brass bells. These bells rang loud and clear, warning others that the motor was coming.

Ken and I waited for the boss to come and take us to our assignment for that night. After all the men had left and the motors had gone inside, we were on our way back into the interior of the mine.

The wide opening near the shaft quickly closed into the main level and main line. A drift, blasted from solid rock measuring about thirteen feet at the bottom and arching to a height of about nine feet, ran far back into the ore body where the actual mining took place. The drift was dimly lit with overhead bulbs spaced far apart. Two sets of air doors controlled the ventilation. One large door was located across the tracks, next to a twelve-foot long passageway for the men to walk through. The "manway" had a small door at each end.

The "manway" was separated from the big door by a concrete wall. As the men passed through the first door, they would close it before opening the second door. This procedure had no effect on the ventilation or air pressure, but with both doors open, the air current and pressure was such that it made walking difficult.

The big doors were operated by air cylinders with steel cables running to a control handle. Approaching motor crews hit the handle to open and close the door. They opened with a loud bang—quicker than any door I had ever seen. It would be a serious injury if you were to get caught between the doors and the side of the drift.

On that first night, I saw something new and different with every step. The boss explained that the iron pipes running along the left side carried the compressed air and water for operating the miners' jack hammers, jack legs, air shovels, and other air-operated machines. On the opposite side, bigger pipes connected to fans carried air into the mine.

We walked along a planked walk over a drainage ditch coming out of the mine. As motors passed, we would stop and lean against the side of the drift to avoid being struck by the cars or motor.

The main drift, I believe, extended more than a half-mile from the shaft. At that point, the drift widened for a few feet. This was where the body of iron ore began and the solid rock ended. Two timbered drifts branched out from the main drift. These drifts went back further into the ore body with other drifts branching out of them.

It was at this junction that my friend and I got formally introduced to the water ditch we walked along and were given our work assignment. We had to clean

71

out the ditch by bailing out all the mud that had settled on the bottom and whatever other debris floated along the drift—uneaten lunch, lunch wrappers, rat carcasses, and human waste. The ditch not only drained water, but served as a toilet in the absence of any other.

The foreman brought out two galvanized pails and shovels from the nearby bosses' shack and told us that the motor crew would be bringing us a buggy to dump the mud/waste. We took turns filling the pails and dumping them into the buggy. Standing in the ditch, the pail could be filled by either scooping or using the shovel. It made little difference whether we were filling or emptying the pail. In either case, it didn't take long to get wet and dirty.

We soon heard and felt the concussion of the miner's blasting. Automatically, we began counting the number of holes that were being blasted. The miners did this to determine if all the holes had detonated, or if there had been a miss-hole. Within minutes, the thick reddish smoke came out of the drift like an oncoming fog bank. As the smoke reached us, we could smell the strong gas from the blast, and sought an area out of the smoke. Throughout the night we heard many blasts from nearby, from further inside, and from above.

Shortly after 7:00 a.m., miners began to group near the bosses' shack to wait for the walk back to the shaft. The boss came and joined the men, and all headed for the shaft and the cage ride to the surface.

We were no longer easily identified as greenhorns. Our clothes were not only dirty, but wet from working in the ditch. I would have sworn that someone had moved the shaft during the last eight hours. The distance between our work place and the shaft seemed to have doubled. Arriving on the surface, I discovered that some miserable bastard had increased the number of steps from fifty-two to at least one hundred. After taking a shower, I headed for home. Even the distance between home and the dry had become longer and the sand cut deeper and steeper to climb.

Breakfast was not time consuming, it was hurriedly eaten. The major concern of the moment was to get into bed and catch up some of the lost sleep from Tuesday night. Sleep did not come on the night before I went to work because of the excitement and anticipation, but after completing my first shift I was dog tired. I felt soreness and stiffness in muscles and bones that I never knew I had.

Yet, in spite of the lack of sleep, the soreness and stiffness, I had a feeling of accomplishment, contentment and confidence. Here I was, exactly one week after my eighteenth birthday, a one-day veteran of working underground. I was feeling content with the opportunity to work among the miners who had come to mean so much to me since childhood. I felt confident that the future would be bright and that I need not want or go without anything I wished for. After all, I had already earned nearly $4.50 for working only eight hours. Many hours of sound sleep followed, ending my first day in the mine.

Family Ties to Iron Ore Mining

When I began working at the Negaunee Mine, it was not uncommon to see men as old as seventy or even older still working. Some had already worked for fifty years, but still held on until their bodies could take no more. Pension benefits were unheard of in 1943 and were but a dream for the miners. Prior to the enactment of the Social Security Act of 1935, the retired had no kind of benefits.

The reason for the long service in the mines was that age was not the primary factor in getting hired. One's size and strength was more important in the earliest days of mining. It is not uncommon to have many members of many generations compile family histories covering hundreds of years of mining experience. The Ronn family is one such family. Family histories do not suggest that its members were or continue to be of any greater importance than the men and women who work their first day and bring a new generation into the mining industry.

Perhaps the only importance to the family with a long history is that its members have had the opportunity to work and listen, not only to their fathers and grandparents, but to others of the same age. They also had the opportunity to listen to their experience of living and working in the mining communities.

Unfortunately I, like many others, have not traced family roots back in time. When plans for the Lake Superior Iron Ore Sesquicentennial were announced, I decided to look back to the time our family first became involved with iron ore mines. I am fortunate to still have an uncle on the Ronn side of the family who has given me information that I never had before.

I had no recollection of my paternal grandfather, Otto Ronn, other than he was mean and abusive to his wife and children. Also, that he was a heavy drinker who butchered cows and pigs for people in the community. For this, he usually took some of the meat from the slaughtered animals to help feed his family.

According to my Uncle Walter, now approaching his 90th birthday, the family came to America in 1892. Leaving their home in Finland close to the Swedish border, Otto and Maria Ronn, with their four daughters and two sons, came directly to Ishpeming. They took residence on Jasper Street where three more boys were born, bringing the number of kids to nine.

Otto went to work in one of the mines in Ishpeming the same year he arrived – 1892. Before his death by pneumonia, he had worked as an underground miner for thirty-nine years, mostly at the Holmes Mine.

Four of Otto's sons also went to work in the mines. Axel worked for fifty years, mining at the Section 16 Mine and Cliff Shaft Mine. My father, Eino, worked for forty-three years as a miner at the Negaunee, Athens, Bunker Hill, and Maas Mines in Negaunee.

Walter wrote me a letter describing his two years underground at the Section 16 Mine. Here is what he wrote:

When I worked in the Section Sixteen
Mine, if you got injured like a broken
leg or arm you had to come on crutches
or a cast on and stay in the dry house
for eight hours so the company did not
have to make an injury report. The
temperature in the Section 16 Mine was
over one hundred degrees. The miners
wanted a fresh air duct put in for fresh
air. (No union – no duct.) All they had
was an air compressor that blew around
the same ore dust and dynamite smoke.

Otto's fourth son, Eskel, worked for a short time
in one of the Cleveland Cliffs Mine offices. He was the
first and only member of our family to have been fired.
Though Eskel lived for only thirty-seven years before
dying after surgery, he made a lot of friends and was
highly respected by workers and farmers. I have only
faint memories of him, because I was only six at the time
of his death in May 1931. I learned from his brothers and
sisters that he was a non-smoker and never drank. This
did not affect his friendship or companionship with those
who did smoke and drink. As a very hard and determined
advocate and organizer of the Central Co-Operative
Movement in the Great Lakes states, he devoted the last
ten years of his life to the cooperative movement.

The Evening Telegraph, a newspaper published in
Superior, Wisconsin, wrote many articles about his life.
Here are some excerpts taken from the Thursday, May 21,
1931, edition:

Flower tributes which were sent by 87
individuals, business firms and co-
operative agencies — reportedly the
floral arrangements cost nearly $2,000
— and practically covered the big
stage.

He had only a common school
education. For a time he worked for

the Consolidated Lumber Company and later for the Cleveland Cliffs Iron Company. Mr. Eskel Ronn was discharged from the mining company because of his beliefs in labor.

He helped to build the co-operative wholesale, not as a one-man organization, but one of collective leadership.

Always knew that whatever proposals Eskel Ronn made, they were not personal whims, but the result of mature thinking and consultation with all department heads.

Eskel never wanted to shine as Eskel Ronn, but always tried to be one of the workers in the organization.

Eskel victoriously carried the banner with the slogan that workers and farmers must themselves control their own affairs without any outside dictation.

Even if mistakes may be made, it is only through their own activities that the worker will learn.

He is gone but there is consolation for us all in the fact that he left a work that will last forever.

Eskel Ronn is dead. His activities are at end. This is the law of nature. We lament only because he died in the prime of his life. However, Eskel is still living among us in the sense that his deeds will not be obliterated.

He paved the way for the co-operative movement. He pioneered the cause of cooperation among the Finns and Americans. In fact, his sudden death was due to his self-sacrificing efforts to the movement at the cost of his health.

The interest and well-being of the workers and farmers demand that they learn to take care and control of their own affairs.

The Tenet of Eskel Ronn was 'do everything to arouse the working class to understand its own power.'

The article ended by reporting that a cortege of more than one hundred automobiles followed the funeral coach and Eskel to the cemetery.

Many accused Eskel of being a Communist, though he was vehemently opposed to Communism. Many local co-op stores and credit unions were visited by Commies demanding an annual fee from every one of their members. This money was to go to the Soviet Union and the Communist Party. Eskel followed the Communist fundraisers, telling the co-op members that not a penny was to be given to any Communist party overseas or in this country.

I have been told by two men that Eskel was definitely not of Communist mind but more of a Socialist. This information came from a Finnish minister and a university professor from Ohio. Both had done a lot of research on the Finnish immigrants that came to northern Minnesota, Wisconsin, and the Upper Peninsula of Michigan.

The most interesting excerpt from the newspaper article was the reference to Eskel being fired by the Cleveland Cliffs Iron Company for his beliefs in labor. I brought this information to one of the Cleveland Cliffs

Industrial Relations Representatives during one of my last negotiations that I participated in with that company. I jokingly asked, "How come you fired my uncle some fifty years ago because of his strong support in unions?" He looked at me and said, "What in the hell good did that accomplish?"

I called Uncle Walter after reading about Eskel's firing to find out more specific information. Eskel always carried a pocket watch, and it was his watch fob that lead to his discharge. On this fob was the official emblem of the I.W.W., the Industrial Workers of the World, often referred to as the Wobblies. Though he was never a member of that organization, it apparently alarmed management enough to fire Eskel.

Two of Otto Ronn's daughters married underground miners. Tyni married Salmon Ristamaa, who was killed in a mine accident in 1918, after working underground for twenty-one years.

In the same letter in which Walter described his experience at the Section Sixteen Mine, he wrote this about Salmon's death:

> I can't remember the name of the mine that Salmon Ristamaa was killed in, it was located about one mile past Ruona's Pop Bottling Shop in West Ishpeming, on the left side of the road going to North Lake. One morning he was going to work and he felt sick, he took his dinner pail as far as the gate and decided to stay home. On the very skip he was to go down on, that skip malfunctioned and plummeted to the ground with forty-eight men on it. Several died and the rest were badly injured. But two weeks later he was crushed by a huge rock while shoveling. His body was so badly damaged his coffin had to be closed.

The second daughter Ellen, married William Roine, who worked for fifty-one years as a miner, mostly at the Cliff Shaft Mine. Unfortunately, with the exception of wife Ellen, all others in the Ronn family have never forgotten or forgiven those few days that he crossed the picket line during the 1946 iron ore strike. This blemished his record and brought himself shame.

The oldest of the three Ristamaa boys, Russell, went to work at the Cliff Shaft Mine and at the time of his retirement, had worked for over forty-eight years as a miner.

Shortly after Otto Ronn and his family left Finland for America, another Otto left Finland. Otto and Ida Marttinen and one daughter arrived in Negaunee and lived on Ann Street. Three more girls were born in this country after their arrival.

Otto went to work at the Negaunee Mine. He was seriously hurt in a mine accident that ended his thirty-six year career as a miner.

His oldest daughter, Hilda, was the only daughter born in Finland. She married one of the three sons of Otto Ronn born in Ishpeming. Hilda Marttinen and Eino Ronn were married in March of 1922. They became my parents on June 15, 1925.

After their marriage, another brother, Axel, married my mother's sister Aune. Both couples lived on Ann Street until their deaths.

A third daughter of the Marttinen family also married an underground miner, John Renfors. Jack, I believe, was a North Lake resident before he married Vienno and moved to Ann Street. Both lived there until they died. Jack worked as a miner and shift boss for forty-seven years at the Negaunee and Mather Mines. Two of the Renfors boys, Ronnie and Richard, also went to work for the Cleveland Cliffs Iron Company.

I worked underground at the Negaunee, Athens, and Bunker Hill Mines for approximately sixteen years before accepting appointment to the position of Staff Representative for the United Steelworkers of America on February 1, 1959.

My son, Jeff, became the fourth generation of the family to work for Cliffs. As a summer student, he worked at the Research Lab, Pilot Plant and with the Surface Survey Crew. During medical school and as an intern, he worked with our family doctor, R.G. Williams. As the Cleveland Cliffs Medical Director, Doctor Williams had Jeff assist in the physical exams of the miners and crew members on the company ore carriers. My daughter Marsha worked for a short period at the Williams Clinic as an office clerk.

On October 1, 1992, the fifth generation began to work in the Cleveland Cliffs operations. My grandson, Todd Ronn, started in the mines nearly a century after his great-great-grandfather Otto Ronn worked his first shift in 1892.

How others look upon this history of two immigrant families spanning so many years with a total in excess of 400 man-years is not important. If we made any contribution, it would be that iron ore mining still continues on the Marquette Range. Though the underground mines and the miners have given way to the big and modern open-pit mines, today's men and women workers and the mine operators enjoy working conditions, wages and benefits, and profits far beyond the wildest dreams of their predecessors.

Hopefully, generations in the distant future will build and continue making the lives of all a little better, safer, and more secure. After all, this is all that previous generations sought. Having had the privilege to be associated with them, I know of no better goal in life than to make life a little better for those who will follow us. In this regard, the Ronn family has tried its best. We have not been, or pretend that our contribution has been any more than any other family's contribution to the iron mining industry. Ours has seen one killed in the mines, another seriously crippled by a mine accident, another fired for union conviction, and, unfortunately, one who even scabbed.

Chapter 5—Fifty-Two Steps

It was less than a month after that first shift underground and five weeks after graduation that most of my curiosity about iron ore mines was satisfied. This curiosity from the earliest of childhood memories began and continued to increase as I got older. As a toddler, I had sat in my uncle's yard or at the end of the avenue, watching how the ore came out of the shaft house and what was involved in shipping the ore out of the mine.

In the summer, I could see the steam shovel loading ore from the stockpiles. Cars were also loaded at the pockets of the shaft. Skips emptied the ore into the pockets and the cars. A car rider would release the brakes on the railcar and ride it down the side tracks where trains would later pick them up. A sampler would walk over the loaded cars and take ore samples for lab testing. A length of rope would be stretched over the length of the car with markings where the samples would be taken. Small cards would be attached to each railcar, indicating the mine from where the ore came. In the off-shipping season, the activity involved taking ore to the stockpile along the trestle that could be seen from a window.

Going along the short cut to elementary school brought me close to the timber yard and other surface areas where men worked. All of this activity added to my growing curiosity.

From my many trips to the mine carrying dinner pails, I had seen close-up activity, the mine shaft, and head frame. By the age of ten, I had been given the opportunity to get a good picture of the surface workings of an underground iron ore mine.

The first eight hours of working at the mine brought many answers to the questions I had, and ended a lot of the curiosity that I had carried for so many years. Along with discovering that there were fifty-two steps on the stairway, I had seen how timber and supplies got underground. The cage ride into the mine showed me a new and darker world.

81

This learning experience involving the mines could be compared to one's formal schooling, but with one major exception. In school, one started at the beginning—in kindergarten. I began the learning process about mines and iron ore at the end of the production cycle when the ore was shipped out. In the short period of a few weeks I was given the chance to complete the cycle of mining iron ore, from the first step of actually mining to the shipment to the ore carriers.

After the first two shifts, my former classmate and I were assigned other work. I was made part of a three-man motor crew on the following Monday. The shift rotations at that time differed from the present day scheduling. Men went from midnight to day, then to afternoon shift.

Where It All Begins

Working on the motor crew brought me back into the farthest reaches of the mine. The naked rock drift from the shaft ended where the iron ore body began and two drifts branched out where the rock ended. Along the sides of the ore drifts, lagging, poles and large timbers were piled between the track and sides of the drift. Supplies would be hoisted up to the miners as needed. Another three-man crew, the timber hoisters, would hoist the miner's supplies up the ladder road compartment of the two-compartment cribbed raise. The second compartment, the dirt road, was used to get the ore down to the level for loading. These cribbed raises were as high as 200 feet, depending on the distance between levels and the size of the ore body.

Most of the main raises up from the level were developed by two-man raise miner contracts. These miners usually worked on the day shift and did all the drilling, blasting and cribbing of the raise. Working on two-inch thick stage planks supported by two stage piles, they worked high above the mine line with nothing but air between them and the tracks below. Using a raise drilling machine and a set of drills, they would blast out five to six feet at one blasting.

82

The run on the drilling machine was about eighteen inches. This required a set of drills varying in size, each drill longer than the last one in the machine. After the blast, one miner would climb back up the raise and prepare for the cribbing that would follow. Mounting a gin, or jim pole, a small block would be attached and the wire rope brought up into the block to hoist the cribbing and blocking from below. Often, drillers used only voice signals until the raise became too high to be heard. Then, a light signal was used.

As the cribbing reached the stage above, it would be put into place and wedged tight to the sides of the raise. These men, accustomed to working together for years, knew each other's moves. The miner on the level knew how to size the cribbing to keep the tops of the cribbing fairly even as they were being put in. He also knew the size of the blocking and when it would be needed. Special wood wedges were cut in the carpenter shop on surface, and brought into the raise for miners to use in tightening the cribbing. For each round of cribbing in a two-compartment raise, eight tamarack cribbings were needed. The diameter of cribbing varied, but it would take about three complete sets for every two feet of raise. The raise miners could handle and install as many as 2,400 or more cribbings in the highest raises.

Raises developed in solid rock were single compartment, installed primarily for ventilation control, secondary escape routes and for traveling between levels. Because of the hard rock, a different drilling machine, drill rods and bits were required. Weighing more than one hundred pounds, the raise machine had a similar run as the smaller machine, and also required a special set of drill rods. These rods were square, with a special bit that was threaded on and off the rod when dull. A hole ran in the center of the rod and through the bit. Because of the hardness and the resulting dust that would come from drilling dry, water was constantly run through the bit as it turned. This kept the bit cool and the dust down. However, this type of drilling in the confined space of a naked raise was of no comfort to miners. Standing only on the narrow stage, they had no place to go to avoid the constant spraying and fog coming out of the holes being drilled above, and the exhaust coming out of the machine. The noise coming from the drilling was deafening in these spaces that were no bigger than most shower stalls.

With many years of experience and working together, raise miners were as skilled as any person in any occupation. Whether they cribbed the raise or not, the lines given them by mining engineers were accurately followed. To look up into the finished raise left no doubt as to their skills. The raise was as straight as an arrow and the designated incline as smooth as possible.

As a crew member, one of my duties was to walk behind the ore train as it was being pushed inside the ore drift for loading. Until the train came to the crosscuts, the motorman would ring the brass bell mounted on the motor. This bell would give a clear and loud signal to men in the main drift that the train was coming. Before entering the ore drift, my job was to walk ahead and warn men working the drift to get out of the way. In the event a timber hoister or other worker had the tracks blocked for some reason, the motorman was signaled to stop. Signals between the motorman and the man walking behind were given by moving his head. By rotating his head in a circular fashion, the beam from the miner's lamp told the motorman to back up. Shaking the head from side to side told him to stop. By moving the head up and down, the motorman started moving the train forward and out of the drift. Once loaded, the train would move to the main line and wait for its turn to go to the pockets to unload.

On one of my earliest walks behind the train, I had to signal the motorman to stop. A timber hoister had a load of poles across the tracks waiting to be hoisted up to the miners. It was Jimmy Jewell, a slightly built elderly veteran of nearly half a century of working underground; age and work had already taken its toll. Still, this quiet Englishman kept working to the best of his ability. In addition to being quiet and soft spoken, Jim seemed to always be in deep thought. Rolling big timbers onto the tracks or making loads of poles and lagging were not easy or light work, even for much younger men. Those in the area where Jim was working always provided a helping hand. Often I wondered how difficult it must have been for this old and tired man to climb the long stairway between the tunnel and the dry. It was not long after my first meeting with Jim that the time had come when any work in the mine had become impossible for him.

Along both sides of the ore drifts were many chutes at the bottom of the ore raises. Opposite the chute was a small loading platform where the brakeman and chuteman operated the chute door to load the ore in the raise into empty cars. After each car was loaded, another empty car spotted until the raise was emptied, or all cars were filled.

The task of loading from the raise ranged from fairly easy to most difficult. Ore that was both dry and fine ran like sugar, and the heavy steel chute door easily opened and closed. Wet ore along with chunky ore sometimes caused real problems. If a large chunk of ore or some other obstacle such as broken cribbing or loose plank wedged between the open door and lip of the chute it caused a "jack pot." Ore would overflow the car and onto the level. Sometimes many tons of ore would have to be cleaned up before the chute could be closed and the mess cleaned up. Large jackpots brought the miners down to the level to help in the clean-up. Shoveling the finest and driest of ore was heavy work in the best of conditions; between the side of the drift and car was not a favorite of the miners or motor crew. The trammer boss was not amused over the delay in getting ore to the shaft, and in his eyes this amounted to a major catastrophe.

The cars were rocker-type and had a load capacity of five tons. To dump the ore into the pockets, the chuteman and brakeman held the handle at each end and unhooked the catch bars. Cars that were well balanced with the load were not hard to turn over. Cars heavily loaded to the pocket side made it difficult to unhook the catch because of the overbalance. Cars loaded heavy on the side where the two workers stood were the heaviest to dump. The overbalanced load sometimes made it necessary to use a length of pipe put on an angle between the plat floor and rib of the car. A pipe held in this position by one man and the motorman would slowly move the train. As the car moved, the pipe began to straighten up, thereby lifting the body of the car to where it turned over when the weight of the ore was overbalanced to the opposite side of the car.

When emptied, the cars had to be pulled back to their upright position. Cars that turned all the way over and off the tracks had to be lifted back on track with the use of a heavy jack and props.

All of the ore brought out of the miner's contracts had samples taken for testing at the company lab. Every car from each contract was credited and written on the tally board. After the last train was dumped, the foreman would mark down the number of cars credited to each of his contracts for that shift.

Big Rats

The men underground had a lot of experiences with big rats that infested the Negaunee Mine. Men who carried their lunch in paper bags had to be careful where they put it. If they left their lunch bag on a plank on the side of the drift, it meant a quick a meal for the rats. Even if they put their lunch in their jacket pocket, it still did not deter the hungry rats. They could easily chew a hole in the jacket to get to the lunch. For the paper bag lunches, the men found that the safest way to protect them was to suspend them on a piece of wire long enough to make it impossible for the rat to reach.

Killing these big rats was a challenge and many methods were tried. Throwing a chunk at them was done mostly in vain, as they were always running or on the move, climbing between the sets of timber. If lucky enough to get one cornered, a steel chute bar or piece of wood might get the rat if the aim was on target. One means of entertainment for the miners, but not for the rat, was to place a saw on the damp or wet ground and place some food on the saw blade. Attaching a piece of wire from the steel blade to the trolley wire completed the stage and preparation for the show. The hungriest rats would immediately smell the food and run onto the electrically charged saw. Both the saw and the rat were usually wet and provided a good contact. Once on the charged saw, the rat squealed and jumped up and down until the momentum carried it off the blade. It would stagger down the drift and into the first hiding place it came to.

Regardless of how many rats might have been destroyed, their numbers seemed to increase. At least one of the older miners suggested that it was futile to kill any rats and that by doing so only increased their number. He believed that the killing of each rat brought at least six more to serve as pallbearers and mourners.

Payday

Before leaving the motor crew, I received my first paycheck. The company paid its workers twice a month at that time. Paydays would be on or near the fifteenth and thirtieth of each month, depending on if the mine was working on that day. A couple days before the actual payday, men had to pick up their due bills from the mine payroll office. These due bills, about the size of a dollar bill, showed the number of hours worked and the rates paid, along with whatever deductions were made.

All of this information was written only in pencil. This was of considerable advantage to some men who never let their wife see the actual check. The man cashed his check and brought the money home to his spouse. The money she received was the exact amount shown on the due bill that he had given her two days earlier. What the wife never knew is that her husband had done a little editing on the due bill. The pencil markings were easy to erase and alter. By adding a power bag, charging stick or some other unchargeable item as a deduction and changing the amount due, the man was able to hide some spending money that his wife would never be aware of.

The pay received was always delayed by one pay period. I received my first check in the middle of July for the seven shifts I had worked in June. Looking at a check made payable to me was only one surprise. To realize that I still had another check coming for nearly twenty-eight dollars for the seven shifts, even after deductions for a safety helmet, lamp belt and one dollar for my first month's insurance premium. After cashing the check, I had more money in my pocket than I ever believed possible. With this new-found wealth, nothing less than being drafted for service in World War II could possibly interfere with a future free of want and free of worry.

Mining

Subsequent to my first payday, I worked on the motors for another week, and met another old-timer. Like Jimmy Jewell, Ed Peterson had also worked many years at the Negaunee Mine. Ed suffered with a double hernia larger than I had ever seen before or since. To support the ruptures, Ed had to wear a heavy leather truss. This required a lot of time both at the start and end of each workday. Leather straps and laces had to be adjusted and properly placed before he could put his mining clothes on. At the end of the shift, the reverse procedure had to be done before he could go into the shower room. Ed was assigned to do a variety of jobs and was regularly scheduled for the day shift. His primary duty was that of a powderman, along with emptying "honey buckets" of human waste, and sharpening miners' axes. A specially built truck enclosed with wood was brought to the entrance of powder rooms throughout the mine. The fifty-pound boxes containing one hundred sticks of dynamite were carried into the powder room, a small opening blasted into solid rock with a wall and entrance door facing the main drift. Ed had to take sticks of dynamite out of the boxes and store them on shelves. Dynamite sticks were separated by the percentage of nitroglycerin they contained. As the miners came to the powder magazine to get dynamite, Ed would fill the powder bag and record the amount of dynamite each contract took. I would guess that in the course of twenty-four hours and with the many mining contracts, the amount of dynamite used ran into a number of tons.

In the event time permitted, Ed would walk along the planked walkway in the main drift and throw sawdust on the slippery surfaces. Many of the older miners predicted that some high official or visitor touring underground would see how much sawdust covered the entire length of the walkway between the shaft and mining area.

Other contract miners, in addition to raise mining, worked in the main levels. These were the rock drift miners who developed drifts through solid rock and in the ore body on the main line. In rock, these men used the heavy water drilling machines and jack legs. Later came the two-man and three-man jumbo drilling rigs. Blasted rock was loaded by air-operated loaders and, in later years, electrically operated loaders. Miners in rock mining worked under noisy and often wet and greasy conditions as they drilled and loaded the rock.

Day shifts had more men on the level and throughout the mine. Pipemen were installing or removing water and airlines, ventilation tubing and pipes. Timber crews were repairing broken sets of timber and installing timber slides and chutes. Other maintenance men were repairing jack hammers and similar tools that could be repaired underground.

Track crews were installing new tracks. Where the tracks had been raised by pressure and twisted, they lowered the rails to keep the motors moving.

After three weeks working on the main line learning that phase of ore production, I moved to the last phase, that beginning point of ore mining that had intrigued me since I was a young kid. This missing link would now be discovered—I would be my father's partner in Contract Number thirty-six! Like his father-in-law taught him many years earlier, my father would now teach me about mining iron ore.

This type of family pairing was very common at that time. Fathers worked with sons, brother with brother, father-in-law with son-in-law, brothers-in-law working together as were all brothers. I believe these combinations were in the interest of both the miners and the company. The family relationship may have led to a greater awareness of safety than it may have in different pairings. Most sons would agree that their fathers were much harder men to work with.

There were many family combinations as contract miners. Among them were Dick Anderson and his son Walter. They worked as our opposite partners when I first went mining. Dick Anderson and all five of his sons —Walter, Herb, Carl, Eugene, and Clement—had long careers working for the company.

A few other family combinations I recall were Selim Jarvi and brother Bernhardt, Vic Sivula and his son "Sippu," the Bianchi brothers from Gwinn, Rudy Holapaa and his brother Art, Ed Peterson and his brother-in-law Nels Anderson, Rudy Johnson and his son Leonard, "Suppi" Saari and his brother-in-law Arne, "Dinky" Carilli and his half brother "Puga" Jacobetti, and John Mackey and his brother Charlie. These men and many other such partners worked at the Negaunee and Athens Mines. Similar combinations, I believe, were at all of the other mines on the range.

Within a few weeks after graduation and my eighteenth birthday, I had actually ridden the cage down into the mine. I had seen the workings on the main drift and along the haulage drifts into the ore body. I had already watched men going about their work as skip tenders, motor crews, trackmen, and pipemen installing ventilation, air and water lines, timbermen repairing in the haulage drifts, timber hoisters, rock drift and raise miners developing new drifts and raises. The number of men working on the main drift varied from shift to shift, the largest crew worked on the day shift.

In late July, I was made a contract miner. One of my first surprises was in climbing the raise up to the work area. What looked so high from the main level was even higher as I climbed the ladders to the top.

While the main level had more men and better lighting in the drift, the miners worked in more isolation. Often the only other men they would see during their shift would be the timber hoister and their foreman. The miners would have only their lamps and a dim light burning above the raise and in the face or breast where they worked. Those who came up to the sub would either signal by tapping on the air line or by flashing the lights by turning the main switch on the level.

As new ore bodies were developed, the miners would drive a drift to adjoining contracts. These would be the travel roads between contracts, providing better air circulation and secondary emergency escape routes. Most important to the miners was to get help in lifting heavy timbers, without climbing down and up the ladders to get help.

From the moment I realized I would be working with my father, I was under no illusion as to what I would be confronted with. My father, like so many of his generation and those of older generations, had no fear of work. Indeed they seemed to thrive on it. On every shift, they seemed to set their goal for those eight hours. If possible and under the right conditions, this target would be to complete a round or cycle. A round meant that the miners would complete drilling, blasting, scrapping out all of the ore and put up and finish a complete set of timbers. Under ideal conditions miners would do more than one round per shift. To reach their target or to make conditions safe, eating lunch took a back seat. Sometimes lunch would not be eaten, but left for the following day when there might be more time.

Growing up and working with my father and grandfather and watching neighbors work, I noticed that they all seemed to share the same philosophy in relation to work. This logic was also evident among the old miners I was now working with. A few examples are:

- My grandfather always claimed that any fool could put two fence posts in a straight line but it took more than a fool to put the third one in line.
- If a man's word is not his bond, he should always carry a pencil and eraser.
- The hardest job is to hide from it and not do it.
- The easiest work is to do the best you can. It may not satisfy others but as long as you do your very best,

you can always look yourself in the mirror without guilt or shame.

- A watch is not too important to carry on the job. Working for yourself, your body will always tell you when to stop. Working for others, someone in charge will tell you when it's time to quit.

Cave-Ins and Other Accidents

As the mined-out areas grew bigger, the pressure and weight increased on the supporting timbers. A drift or slice that started out as an arch some thirteen feet wide at the bottom and tapered to about eight feet at the top and eight feet high, gradually got pushed in and down.

Experienced miners could often sense when a drift or part of it might come down. Although the creaking of lagging was usual, the sound tended to become louder and more sustained. Small chunks would start to fall between the covering in the sides and in the back of the drift. Soon, timbers would start to shake slowly, then faster, much like an earthquake, except the danger came from both sides and over the miner's head. When this occurred, the miners quickly got the hell out of the work area and into a safe place. This might mean going into a neighboring contract or down into the ladder road.

Soon the pressure and weight would break down the drift, causing a rush of air and dust. Only when they returned to the drift did the miners know the extent of the destruction. Sometimes only a few sets would come down, but on other occasions the entire drift would collapse. The amount of ore left behind determined whether or not the drift should be repaired.

Unfortunately, there were times when miners weren't aware of an imminent cave-in. This resulted in the miners being trapped or buried. Whenever this occurred, other miners were brought in to rescue the men inside. Tapping on air lines, the rescuers waited for a signal from the trapped miners. Though important to get to the men as fast as possible, care had to be taken to avoid further cave-ins or injury to the men involved in the rescue.

One such cave-in, many years prior to my time, was often talked about by the old miners. Two miners, Vic Sivula and his partner, reportedly were trapped between the breast and the cave-in. After many hours of working to clear a hole, they were told it was okay to come out, but to be careful to avoid another fall of ground. As the rescuers anxiously waited, the first thing they saw coming out was a jack-hammer. It was followed by Vic who was pushing the drilling machine ahead of him. When asked why he was more concerned with the machine than himself, Vic replied, "This is too good of a jack-hammer to leave behind."

Vic Vaisinen was one of the legends of the past. Vic apparently felt best when he had a shovel in his hand, shoveling iron ore. At the Negaunee Mine, there were standing orders to get Vic back to the mine whenever a cave-in occurred and men were trapped. Vic was given the nickname of "Steamshovel" because of his ability to move a lot of dirt over a long period with his shovel.

Cave-ins and falling ore rock were only two of the hazards confronted by the underground workers. Serious injury or death was also a possibility when handling dynamite or machinery. Falling down a high raise was another type of accident. Perhaps the most feared, and involving many men, was an underground fire where smoke, heat, and gases made escape difficult at best, or worse impossible. Here on the Marquette Iron Range, Cleveland Cliffs had a special and highly trained crew of miners to fight underground fires. The Athens Mine had at least two such fires that were successfully put out by this crew. As a boy I often saw these men walking along the road in the heat of summer, wearing their gas masks and carrying the heavy air packs on their backs.

One of the ways men were warned of impending danger and to leave their work areas was the use of a foul-smelling chemical or other substance in the main air lines coming from the surface. Soon the entire underground smelled something much worse than rotten cabbage and a hundred skunks. To avoid evacuation of the mine, a test of the system took place before miners were notified in advance.

Many of the older miners told stories about accidents and deaths that occurred in earlier times. Most, I believe, were just tales to let the rookie know that many men could be killed or hurt. One story involved a man killed immediately upon arriving in his work area. The undertaker was called to the mine to pick up the body. The hearse of that day was only a horse-drawn wagon. When the corpse was brought up from underground and put into the hearse, the teamster made no move to take the body to the morgue. When asked what he was waiting for, he answered that he was going to wait for a full load.

On another occasion, two men were seriously injured underground and the horse-drawn ambulance was called out to the mine. When the injured men were put into the ambulance, the driver made no effort to rush them to the hospital. When asked what he was waiting for, he answered that the horses were eating, and as soon as they finished he would take the men to the doctor.

In the early days of mining there was a practice of shutting down the mine after a man lost his life. It remained shut down until the day after his burial. Because of the number of men killed, miners seldom got to work for a full half (half of a month). One old timer claimed it got so bad that one miner hid the body of his partner for three days in order to work all of his scheduled days in that half of the month before reporting his death.

There is no question that these tough old miners seldom sought professional treatment except for the most serious injury. Two old Finns that had mined together for many years, Mike Pekkola and Nestor Holms, both had bald spots on top of their heads. One had a chunk fall on his head, causing a fairly large cut. While he sat on a nail keg, his buddy decided to stop the bleeding. He held a length of fuse over the bleeding cut, while holding his burning carbide lamp under the end of the fuse. The heat from the flame melted the protective tar in the fuse, and the hot tar dripped onto the cut.

As this was happening, the mine captain, superintendent and the general manager came into the contract. Mr. Elliot, I believe, was the general manager. After seeing the melted tar being used to stop the bleeding, he couldn't believe his eyes. Seeing the mixture of red blood and the black tar running down the miner's head he asked, "What in the hell are you up to? You have to go to the surface and get that cut taken care of." Mike looked at the official and asked, "You be for doctor?" Mr. Elliot responded, "Of course I'm not a doctor." Mike told him to shut up, and continued caring for his partner. The manager shook his head and left, saying something to the effect that they were both barbaric.

Though I have no recollection of meeting Nestor, I remember Mike very well. Mike was a solidly built man who always had a devilish glint in his eyes. He would often come to me and put his ham-sized fist under my nose in a threatening manner and ask me in Finnish if I was afraid. The friendly threat would end and we would begin talking about many things including his asking how my grandfather was doing. Mike and my grandfather had been friends for many years but the injury to my grandfather ended this close relationship.

Mike and Nestor had a regular act they would put on whenever a man came into their contract for the first time. Both men would grab an ax or pick and begin shouting and cursing each other in Finn, making it look as though they meant to kill each other. After carrying on like this and noticing the startled look on the newcomer, they would laugh and put their arms around each other to bring a sigh of relief from the startled visitor.

Underground Conditions

Miners were often confronted with something similar to a cave-in, caused by a heavy fall of ground or pressure. After blasting, the miners would return to the work area only to discover that the blast had knocked down ore or more sets of timber. This could occur for a variety of reasons, such as the spragues knocked out by a flying chunk of ore, a mishole that caused the charged holes to detonate out of sequence, or multiple holes detonated because of a crack in the breast that could detonate more than one hole at a time. Whatever the cause, in the case of either a cave-in or by blasting, the result was the same. What had taken the miners only hours to install would take days or even weeks to repair, depending on the conditions.

Sometimes a rock run or an unseen seam of water would come through, causing most miserable circumstances. To stop a rock run required not only extreme caution, but patience and time. To add to this, any water would make the rock muddy and more difficult to stop. In wet conditions, miners would wear heavy rubber "oilers" over their regular mining clothes. The work to repair these damaged areas was paid at the "company account" rate, the bare minimum rate. Though the work was difficult and under miserable conditions, miners worked with no incentive rate as they had when they performed the work originally.

Some miners referred to these conditions, the difficult work, and the lack of an opportunity to earn higher pay, as similar to a whore's worst dream. I never knew what a whore's worst dream was. Perhaps it was after working hard serving her patrons, she dreamt that she had to pay her customers, rather than them paying her.

Repair work in any area of the mine was not easy. Travel roads that once stood thirteen feet wide at the bottom and tapered to about eight feet wide at the top and the same height, were crushed and pressed to where miners could no longer travel through. When necessary to keep even a small passage open, repairmen came in to enlarge the opening. Battista Carello, a slightly built Italian, was well known for this type of work. He worked on his knees or stomach, chopping, sawing and shoveling his way through until it became possible for men to crawl through their work areas. Battista worked tirelessly and often in hot and humid places, but he was never known to take a drink of water while underground.

Cribbed raises that were so straight after the raise miners completed them were not exempt from breaking down and in need of major repair. After the raise miners completed their work, others would come and put in the timber slide, safety gates, landing gate, install planks on the two sides, and in the hanging of the ladder road. The timber slide was made of hardwood planks, making it easier to hoist supplies up the raise. Safety gates were made of poles that were spaced at intervals along the ladder road. These gates were mounted and anchored with hinges to stop a person from falling all the way down to the level below. As the loads were pulled up, they pushed the safety gates open to permit the load to go through. Properly balanced, they would drop back into position after the load passed. A landing gate was put in near the top of the ladder road. The load would be lowered onto the gate after it had gone through and the gate had closed. This made it possible to prepare the load to be pulled out of the raise and into the travel road or miners drift.

Nothing would be done immediately to the dirt roadside until after the ore had been scraped into the raise. The ore falling down the raise would wear down high spots on the cribbing. Three-inch-thick hardwood planks would be nailed into the foot of the raise. It would be planked solidly from side to side. Fewer planks were put on the other sides because they were not subject to the same pounding and wear as the foot.

Even when the raise was new, this work was not one of the most enjoyable tasks of the miners. While standing on a ladder or a single plank, the long planks would be raised. Using heavy eight inch or longer spikes, the planks would be anchored into the tamarack cribbing. Even though ore had been dumped into the raise, these heavy planks never rested flat against the cribbing. Using his back and legs, one man would try to force the plank against the cribbing, while his partner drove spikes along the plank until it rested as solidly as possible against the cribbing. Four men worked on this job. Along with the two men in the raise, one would be on the level to hook on the planks, and the fourth man was on top running the air tugger to pull the plank up to where the others were working.

In time, the ground pressure on the sides of the raise would begin squeezing the raise. Soon the safety gates would be useless and the planks in timber slide began to break. The ladders that once were so straight now began to twist and come loose. The ore side of the raise would suffer similar damage, making repair necessary. Like the cave-ins on drifts knocked down by blasting, the repairing of raises was another situation best described as a whore's worst dream. In many cases water ran along the raise, making the tools, planks and replacement cribbing slippery. A heavy rubber coat and pants were necessary to keep dry.

After I started work, the company tried other ways to protect and eliminate the wear on the ore roads. Strips of heavy steel nailed over the planks helped for awhile. Because of the pressure, later the steel strips would come loose and fall crossway into the raise or down against the chute. Ultimately, the repair of the raise became even more difficult, as not only the broken planks and cribbing had to be removed, but the steel plates. This might require the use of acetylene torches. Much later (but not while I was in the mine), heavy steel liners were used. I believe the round sections installed between the cribbing kept the raise in better shape for a longer period of time than the other methods.

Lunch Time

Miners ate mostly in groups when they were on the same mining subs. Timber hoisters and timbermen in the area would also join them. A travel road away from the smoke and gas of blasting was the best lunchroom.

One of the first lessons of a greenhorn was to be told by the older men not to sit on the damp ground. To avoid this and the threatened hemorrhoids resulting from the dampness, every man used a "dry ass." This could be a piece of cardboard from an empty dynamite box or piece of dry plank. The miners would save these protective seating pieces and store them in a dry place until the next lunch time.

It was during lunchtime that I began to hear stories and experiences of the older generation. It also brought other questions to my attention. For example, I am still puzzled by how the miners escaped and survived during the days when they had only candles or carbide lamps to see by. Surely the rush of air coming from a cave-in would blow out any flame from either a candle or carbide lamp. Those trapped behind a cave-in would have to remain in complete darkness without additional candles, carbide or even a match. Nobody can fully realize complete and perfect darkness until they've gone into an underground mine area and turned off the lights, candles, or lamp. How anyone could find his way out of the mining sub without any kind of light had to be next to impossible under any circumstances.

Stories from a Mine

At the time of the closing of the Negaunee Mine, I went to the Athens Mine. The only difference was that the Athens Mine was only two blocks away from my house, in a different direction. As the surface around the Athens Mine began to sink, the company built a new temporary dry next to the sidewalk along Ann Street. The Negaunee Mine shaft was sunk deeper and the mine was renamed the Bunker Hill Mine. At a later date, the Maas Mine, not far north of the Negaunee Mine, was closed down and those employees came over to the Bunker Hill Mine to change clothes and shower. All of the three former, older mines were now operating from a single, newly named company and mine, the Bunker Hill Mine.

Iron ore, under the best conditions, is very heavy. When it is fine, it is easiest to shovel. Chunky ore is much more difficult. Experienced miners, during the days of hard shoveling, could shovel over either shoulder and in the most awkward positions. Before blasting, planks would be placed near the breast and ore falling onto this solar was easier to shovel because of the planks. At times, some contracts were called "one-man shoveling."

Miners would take turns filling the buggy and pushing it to the raise for dumping. One related contract brought complaints from a man working as a stemmer with John Kuvilla. Jimmy Warren was filling in for John's regular partner. When the mine captain came into the contract area, this slightly built Englishman complained that he was "doing all the bloody work" himself. The captain was surprised to hear this because he knew that Big John was one of the hardest working miners, or a rooter, as men like him were referred to. Captain Ware stayed and watched as John quickly filled the buggy and returned it to the ore pile after emptying it. As Jimmy took his shovel and turn at filling the buggy, the captain immediately noticed that it took Jimmy four or five times longer to fill the buggy. To Jimmy, this only meant that he was doing most of the bloody work.

The miners of that era were confronted with a pile of ore after each blast. These piles had to hand-shoveled. Many cars would have to be loaded before the timber was installed and drilling could take place for the next round. An average of fifteen to twenty cars could be expected from each blast, which would amount to between seventy-five and one hundred tons of ore.

During the depression years of the late 1920s and early 1930s, miners were sometimes called out to fill railroad cars by hand, shoveling out of the stockpile. My father and grandfather were called out to do this by moving the ore from the stockpile into the railcar by wheelbarrow along a planked stage. This method was used due to the limited order and demand to fill a special need. Paint ore, used by paint manufacturers, was a special grade of ore and was handled to keep it separated from other ores.

Prior to the introduction of air-operated jack hammers, mines had only a star bit attached to a steel rod to drill holes for blasting. These rods came in various lengths. Miners would begin with the shortest rod. As the hole deepened, longer rods would be used. This was a two-man operation, with one man holding the rod and turning it as his partner kept pounding with a heavy

Portion of Ann Street location with Athens Mine trestle in background.
Negaunee, Michigan

Park Street School, c.1930. Negaunee, Michigan. Ernie –top row, third from left.

Scraper of slusher, looking toward blockhead. 1930's. Marquette Range

Miners drilling underground. 1950's. Marquette Range.

Athens Mine showing head frame and trestle on right and hoist on left. 1918.
Negaunee, Michigan

Source: Cleveland Cliffs Iron Co.

Negaunee Mine timber yard with Ann Street company houses in background. 1913.
Negaunee, Michigan.

Source: Cleveland Cliffs Iron Co.

Ernie Ronn during World War II.
Source: Ernie Ronn

Steps of Negaunee Mine leading up to Dry House.
Source: Ernie Ronn

Ida and Otto Martinnen in front of Chatham farm house.
Source: Ernie Ronn

Ernie Ronn's paternal grandparents, Otto and Marie Ronn.
Source: Ernie Ronn

Timber Set

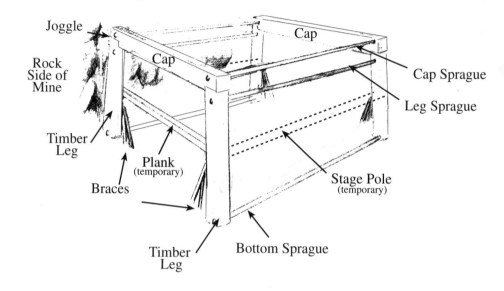

Joggle

Rock Side of Mine

Cap

Cap

Cap Sprague

Leg Sprague

Timber Leg

Plank (temporary)

Braces

Stage Pole (temporary)

Timber Leg

Bottom Sprague

Dynamite Detonation Sequence.
NEGAUNEE MINE

125-150 sticks of dynamite were used. The detonation sequence began with holes #1 and #2 and the rest followed. The bottom portionwas most heavily loaded with dynamite so that the result would be a pile of rock and ore after the detonation.

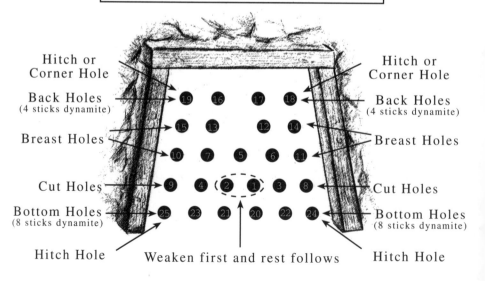

Hitch or Corner Hole

Back Holes (4 sticks dynamite)

Breast Holes

Cut Holes

Bottom Holes (8 sticks dynamite)

Hitch Hole

Hitch or Corner Hole

Back Holes (4 sticks dynamite)

Breast Holes

Cut Holes

Bottom Holes (8 sticks dynamite)

Hitch Hole

Weaken first and rest follows

Block Cave Mining

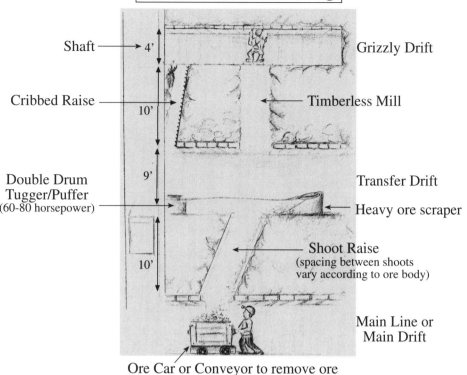

Shaft — 4'

Cribbed Raise — 10'

9'

Double Drum
Tugger/Puffer
(60-80 horsepower) —

10'

Grizzly Drift

Timberless Mill

Transfer Drift

Heavy ore scraper

Shoot Raise
(spacing between shoots
vary according to ore body)

Main Line or
Main Drift

Ore Car or Conveyor to remove ore

Double-Cribbed Raise

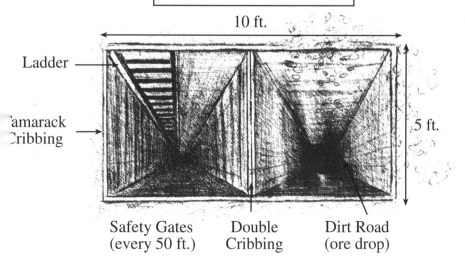

10 ft.

Ladder

Tamarack
Cribbing

5 ft.

Safety Gates
(every 50 ft.)

Double
Cribbing

Dirt Road
(ore drop)

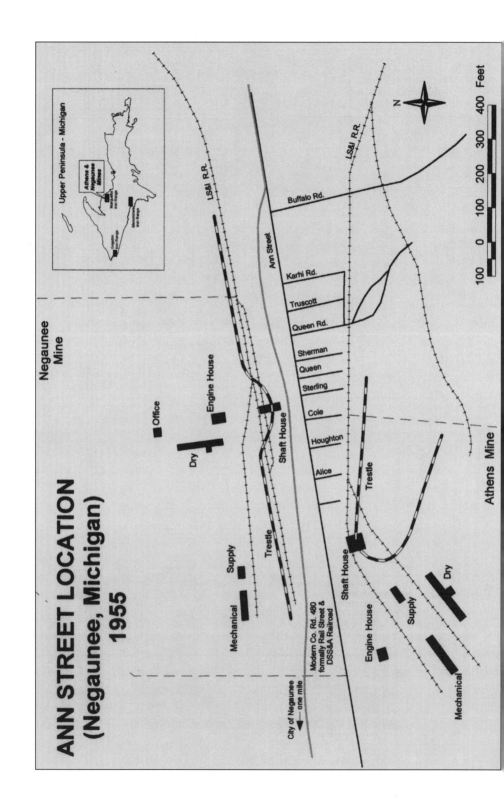

ANN STREET LOCATION (Negaunee, Michigan) 1955

Upper Peninsula - Michigan

Athens & Negaunee Mines

Marquette Iron Range

Gogebic Iron Range

Menominee Iron Range

Negaunee Mine

Office

Dry

Engine House

Supply

Mechanical

Trestle

Shaft House

LS&I R.R.

Ann Street

Buffalo Rd.

Karhi Rd.

Truscott

Queen Rd.

Sherman

Queen

Sterling

Cole

Houghton

Alice

City of Negaunee
← one mile

Modern Co. Rd. 480
formally Rail Street &
DSS&A Railroad

Shaft House

Trestle

Engine House

Supply

Dry

Mechanical

Athens Mine

LS&I R.R.

N

100 0 100 200 300 400 Feet

hammer. One time I spent a half-day with my neighbor using this kind of rod. Simon Chetto, who had used such a rod during his early days, had one. As Simon held the rod, I kept hitting it for hours to drill one hole through a concrete wall. How many hours, indeed days, were necessary before the miners had drilled enough holes to make each blast? The same tools were used to break up the large chucks of ore that were impossible to handle.

One of my first contacts with miners from different mines came on a hunting trip when I was fourteen. In addition to my father and uncle, Walfred Prusi and Freddie Beauchaine were hunting with us in the Big Bay area. All four men were miners from the Athens, Maas, and Negaunee Mines. After the day's hunting would come to an end, we would sit on the edge of a platform made of poles and boughs that served as our bed. In the dim light of a kerosene lamp, I listened to stories of Walfred working at the Athens Mine and of Freddie working at the Maas Mine. The bonds between these four men were strong and lasted throughout their lives.

The Bosses

Though the roles and responsibilities of the miners, bosses, and managers varied, there always seemed to be an understanding between them and very seldom did the bosses or other management attempt to tell the experienced miner how he should go about doing his job safely and effectively. It was a direct insult and left bitter feelings when someone with little or no actual experience in mining would tell an old miner how he should work. While the trained engineer and surveyors had their perspective qualifications and responsibilities as to laying out the direction a miner should go, they knew enough not to tell them how to get there. Once the engineer had put in the lines and/or grade sticks, his job was done.

The top management official at each mine was the mine superintendent. They also showed integrity and respected the ability of the old miners to get the job done and to do it well. The immediate boss had been a miner and had worked for many years alongside the very men he now looked over. If confronted with a danger that had not been experienced before, the boss and the miner would put their heads together to find a way to make it safer.

Some of the early mine superintendents, who had the respect of their employees, were Stan Sundeen at the Cliff Shaft, Henry Moulten at the Maas Mine, and Jimmy Westwater at the Mather Mine. There were others at that time who had deserved and earned this respect but unfortunately their names are not remembered. Over the years, there have and continue to be, men in similar positions who were respected by the miners.

Mr. Graf was mine superintendent at the Negaunee Mine, and as I recall, at the Princeton Mine. As a kid I was impressed by his home. He was considered a very frugal man, not only in his personal life but he was also very tight in managing the mines.

During the Great Depression of the late 1920s and early 1930s, a laid-off old miner, Matt Maki, kept coming to Mr. Graf in the hopes of getting a job, any kind of job at the mines. Mr. Maki was the breadwinner in a very large family and always told Mr. Graf of the difficulty in providing adequate food for them. Mr. Graf could not find any work, but yet tried to be sympathetic to the concerns of the old man. He told Mr. Maki that he too was finding it hard to feed his wife and himself during these trying times. As a matter of fact, Mr. Graf claimed that his family lived on at least one meal of oatmeal every day.

In time the mines began to operate and Mr. Maki returned to work underground. Shortly after he came back, Mr. Graf came underground to inspect the conditions resulting from a long period of inactivity. He came upon Mr. Maki and another miner who were in the process of putting up an unusually large timber to prop up a caving back. Mr. Graf, impressed with the size of the timber, was confident that it would last a long time and save the cost of replacing it. He told Mr. Maki about his confidence in him. Remembering the story about the oatmeal, Mr. Maki said to the mine superintendent, "This would never have gotten into place by just eating oatmeal."

While Mr. Graf ran the Negaunee Mine operations, the mine produced iron ore at record-breaking levels. On one occasion when my father went to pick up his due bill, Mr. Graf happened to be looking out the window at the tram cars dumping ore onto the stockpile. Noticing my father, Mr. Graf told him of the terrible circumstances which confronted him. The railroad hadn't brought in ore cars to be loaded from the pockets, making it necessary to dump the ore on the stockpile. This meant the added costs of later taking it off the pile with a steam shovel.

Mr. Graf asked out loud what, if anything, he could do to avoid this double handling and expense. My father suggested that the problem could be easily avoided by simply picking up the telephone to the underground and telling the skip tenders and motor crews to take a five. This was not the kind of solution he was looking for.

Based on the comments of many men, there was only one mine captain in the early days who was not respected by very many miners at the Negaunee Mine. Though I never met Captain Ware, he reportedly disciplined many, including firing some for little or no reason. Apparently, he regularly walked down Iron Street on Saturday nights or on paydays seeking free drinks from the miners. Failing to buy a drink or ignoring him would result in either a lay-off or discharge. At one point, Superintendent Graf called him into the office and told him that he was fired, and to take his belongings from the mine.

Ware stood in disbelief and came near to tears. He asked why he was being fired and pleaded to keep his job. As he was about to leave the office, he was called back and was asked how it felt to be fired for no reason at all. Mr. Graf reversed his position only after advising the captain that he now knew how the men felt that he had fired for no legitimate reason. He warned Ware that unless he changed his ways, the next time would be final.

Even though the captain had earned the disrespect and scorn of most men under him, he must have had at least one friend. At the time of his retirement, a collection was being passed to purchase a gift for him. When Heikki Harju was approached for a contribution of fifty cents, he asked, "Are you sure the bastard is going to retire?" When told that he was, Heikki pledged a full dollar "just to get rid of him."

At the time I began work, Dick Cattron was the mine captain at the Negaunee Mine. Dick came from England and had a long career in the mines. He was a man who liked to joke and have friendly arguments with the miners. As an Englishman, or more specifically, Cornish, he was proud of being a "Cousin Jack" which on occasion resulted in these friendly confrontations.

During World War II the mines were working a full-time schedule to meet the country's military requirements. Men were regularly scheduled for six days of work every week, with a lot of additional overtime. One man who didn't always report to work as scheduled was Toivo "Muck" Kalmi. Because of his absenteeism, Captain Cattron approached Muck underground, questioning Muck's patriotism and loyalty to the nation during the time of war. Muck apparently was aware of this possibility and was prepared for any questions. He reminded Cattron of how many days he didn't report for work. Cattron's schedule didn't require him to work but a half day on Wednesdays and Saturdays. His position on the city council, board of review, and as city mayor also took him away from the mine on several occasions.

Cattron told Muck that as he came down the gang plank in New York after arriving in America that a voice from heaven told him to "go to the ore mines in Northern Michigan, where fortune awaits you." This didn't have the best effect on Muck, and worsened more when the proud Englishman boasted about the bravery and victories of the British Army in the battles of World War II.

This brought an immediate response from Muck. He asked Cattron if he was aware of the young Englishman who volunteered for service in the American

104

Army. Muck told him that after entering the doctor's office for his physical exam, the recruit was asked to remove his shoes and socks and to drop his pants and underwear. The young man was told to show the bottoms of his feet to the doctor and to bend over and spread his cheeks for examination of his rectum. This took only a few seconds. The doctor told him to put his clothes back on, that he had passed.

The man looked at the doctor and said, "I thought you Yanks had a strict examination of your military men." The doctor agreed that in examining most recruits, a much stricter and complete physical was given. However, with the Cousin Jacks, such an exam wasn't required. Both the man's feet and asshole were in good shape, and he would be able to shit and run when the enemy was confronted. This ended their discussion, and to my knowledge neither man ever again talked of absenteeism or patriotism.

Dick Cattron was a man in the right place at the right time when he was made captain of the Negaunee Mine. The mine, with its ore body, work crew and overall condition, would not have been difficult for any man to assume the captain position.

The captain had a fairly good sense of humor and liked to joke and talk with the men. One habit he had was to tell someone, "goes on, goes on, your cock is out", whenever he thought someone was leading him on. One of the older men he joked with was Simon Maki. Simon was in his mid-to late-sixties and nearing the end of his working years. Dick put his hand on Simon's shoulder and asked Simon how his sex life was and how often he had sex. The old man thought for a moment and told Cattron that he had sex about four or five times a week. In his usual manner, the captain told Simon "goes on, goes on, your cock is out."

Simon, who always wore a heavy mustache, looked the captain straight in the eyes and asked if he wasn't doing enough work as he always had. This concerned the captain and made him feel that he had hurt Simon's feelings by his remarks. He told Simon that he had always been one of the hardest workers in the mine and that no one could ever question this. Again, the old man paused for a second or two, then asked Cattron if he looked like a stupid old fool, and that he would give up sex before cutting back on his work. Simon continued his hard work as long as he remained at the mine. When and how long thereafter did he start cutting down on his sex, nobody knows.

There was another characteristic about Captain Cattron. He usually walked along the main drift with the lamp cord and light draped over his shoulder rather than attached to his hard hat. As he walked he would turn the light from side to side along the ground; whether this was unintentional or intentional, it gave a signal to others that he was coming. I believe that it was not by accident that he did this, but a subtle way to warn anyone who might be smoking a cigarette. Smoking was a severe violation that had only one penalty—discharge.

Smoking Underground

Long before I went to work, there was no penalty for smoking underground. The policy was later changed to the automatic firing of any man caught smoking. I remember hearing stories of how the men reacted after the ban on smoking was first put into effect. One account was that when they came to the surface for lunch, some ate a pack of cigarettes without lighting them.

Whether smoking underground was ever a serious fire threat was an argument that prevailed for years. When miners had only candles or carbide lamps for light they were allowed to smoke. This meant at least three open flames and the possible source of fire where every smoker worked. Subsequently, with the broad use of steel in the mines that required much use of acetylene torches, the fire hazard increased. Yet, novices in the proper use of these torches such as I was, used them in both dry and wet conditions. Men argued and wondered why, if fire was such a hazard, inexperienced men were allowed to use the torches. Some of the management argued the high cost or even impossibility of buying insurance coverage if men were permitted to smoke. This left the question of

106

whether any insurance was carried when the candles and carbide lamps were used.

If the basic reason for this tough restriction was for other reasons such as keeping the miner working instead of relaxing for a few minutes with a cigarette, it was a complete failure. Clandestine smoking and the fear of getting caught took men far away from their work area —places where the ventilation was good and where anyone coming could be seen. Had the men been allowed to smoke in their regular work areas, or at designated lunch times, I believe it would have benefited both miner and management.

The automatic discharge for smoking was later modified, but only after a two-week strike. An incident at the Athens Mine led to the firing of one man which involved a temporary boss and a millrunner. This was what triggered the walkout at the mine and later spread to all the mines on the Marquette Range and into the Mesabi Range of Minnesota. It ended when a three-stage system of penalties for smoking underground was agreed upon. Men would no longer be subject to immediate firing, but would receive a two-week layoff for the first offense, followed by a thirty-day layoff and ultimately a discharge for the third offense.

In retrospect, and with the advantage of 20/20 hindsight and the current wave throughout the country against smoking, it might be interpreted as management's concern for the worker's health, not the fire prevention. If that was true, the argument against smoking would have been more acceptable and understandable, had today's statistics and information been known.

Working under Captain Cattron were three second captains—Wilfred "Greyhound" Tippett, Bill "Bubble Gum" Treloar, and Rubin Carlson. The three men rotated on a three-shift schedule the same as the miners. Their responsibilities covered all of the men and work throughout the mine. It was their job to measure the raises or drifts at the end of each pay period. Miners in development work had their incentive pay calculated on the number of feet the raise or drift was advanced during the half month that covered the pay period. Miners who were mining ore had their rates of pay based on the average number of cars produced per shift during the period. Down time, or company account, was calculated by determining the hourly rate in all cases.

The second captains also had to periodically check their maps and other instruments to make any corrections in the work area.

Wilfred Tippett was given the nickname of "Greyhound" because of the fast pace he walked and climbed raises. Bill Treloar was called "Bubble Gum" because he always chewed gum rather than snuff or Peerless, the choice of most who chewed. Rubin was a more extroverted man than Bubble Gum, who was more introverted and quiet. Rubin liked the outdoors and enjoyed talking about hunting and fishing with the men.

After the mine captain and second captains came the shift bosses who had the day to day contact with their separate crews. At the Negaunee Mine, I recall bosses Abel Laitinen, Gus Jokinen, Bill Hares, Ed Anderson, Bill Tresedder, "Pooke" Laitinen, Bill Denny, and others who I cannot remember by name.

Abel and Gus were in charge of the motor crews, timber hoisters and some mining contracts. Both men spoke their native language Finnish perfectly. They spoke broken English with enough perfection to communicate with their men. Because of their responsibility to keep the ore trains moving, they were referred to as trammer bosses. Between them they had a running contest as to the number of loader cars that would be hauled to the shaft and hoisted during their shift. Whatever the number of cars hauled on Abel's shift had to be exceeded if anyway possible by Gus and his crew who followed. This rivalry was always there until they retired.

Not only were the number of cars a critical issue, but the ore samples were equally important. As samples were taken from all contracts to determine iron and silica content, an overall sampling was also taken. The two trammer bosses, like others in mine supervision, were

108

always aware of the individual contract samplings and the overall sample. All were aware of any special orders or requirements as to the immediate grades of ore for the customers. With this information Abel and Gus, much like expert bakers or lab technicians, knew how to get the right mixture at the right time. High quality ore could be mixed with lower grade ore and by combining them at the right ratio provide the quality being sought.

In the performance of their job, both of these old bosses had their way of communicating with the men. Gus Jokinen had Rudy Johnson and his partner as one of his mining contracts. Rudy was known for his hard work and had few equals in iron ore mining. One morning after a couple hours of starting time, Gus came to John Laukka, a member of the timber hoisting crew and said, "See Johnny, best you not go into Rudy's place. Rudy said he is going to kill the timber hoisters."

John told Gus, "We already been there the very beginning of the shift and hoisted three loads of lagging along with timber and poles." Gus responded that, "When you hoist for Rudy you don't count the number of loads but how many cords you hoisted."

Gus apparently did a lot of reading and on occasion tried to impress others about his knowledge of current issues. He would tell others that "I see by the Chicago Tribune..." of some news article. Whether Gus could read much of an English newspaper remains unknown. One timberman who was an avid reader of newspapers and books was Bill Mattson. One of the papers he routinely read was the Chicago Tribune, and when Gus told him about what he had seen in this paper, Bill advised Gus that he read the same paper and never saw the article Gus referred to. Gus remained silent and a few days later came back to Bill and mentioned something he read the previous night in the Baltimore News. Bill naturally could make no response as he had never seen or heard of this Baltimore paper. I doubt whether there was at that time, or since then, such a paper. It is highly doubtful that a copy has ever been seen in Negaunee. Gus was the obvious winner in this matter.

Abel, like Gus, never showed any inclination to cut short anyone's lunch period or to needlessly criticize. If he thought a motor crew overstayed their 20 minute lunch period, he would pace up and down spitting out Peerless juice. Wondering out loud enough for the crew to hear, he would voice concern that some miners would be coming down to raise hell because the chute was full.

Isadore Lequia, a long time motorman, one day had one of the biggest apples I ever saw in his lunch. As he sat gnawing on this apple, he kept his eye on Abel who was doing his routine, and finally gave up on the fruit and went to his motor. Abel, relieved of his anxiousness, hurriedly told the crew that he would walk behind the train to a loaded chute.

The skips would keep hoisting until the very last minute and stop only when the men began to load on the cage. The telephone or the plat was the only quick way to contact the landing crew on surface. At the end of the afternoon shift, Abel was asked to call the landing and get the score of the basketball game between Negaunee and Ishpeming high schools. These schools have always had a strong rivalry between them, much like that between the two trammer bosses. Abel went to the phone and rang the signal to the landing. While he was doing this the last loaded train was being dumped into the pockets to keep the skips running a few more minutes. He was heard asking, "Who win for ball game?" As he got the answer he turned and said, "Rah-rah," and stopped when he saw one of the ore cars turned off the tracks and laying on its side over the pocket.

Though he originally intended to convey the good news to the supporters of the Negaunee team by completing the message by saying, "Rah-rah Negaunee won," the derailed car was much more critical. He looked at the motor crew and asked, "Who is the pimp that done this?" Accident or not, in his mind nothing short of a pimp would have interrupted the loading of the final skips regardless of how innocent he might have been.

The majority of the bosses had some ability to communicate with their workers. Some spoke fluent

110

Swedish, Italian or Finn and had no difficulty in talking to the men who knew the same language. Others had the capability of reaching and understanding the men with very little ability to speak the English language.

Bill Denny was a rather tall and lanky Englishman. He was one of those men who always appeared to be in need of a shave. He was well liked and highly thought of by every man in the mine. Bill was easily identified by the ragged and torn mining clothes he wore. He along with an old Finn by the name of Heikki Harju picked out the old clothes from the barrels where they had been discarded by the original wearer. Others joked about the clothes both men wore, saying they feared they could be beaten to death by the shredded jackets if ever they were caught between two open air doors. Heikki, who had been a widower for many years, it was fun to watch as he put on his socks. Seldom did any one sock pair up with another, either in size or material. Every sock had holes in it. As each sock was put over another, Heikki had to twist and turn it so that one hole didn't come directly over another. It was not unusual for Heikki to have as many as three or four layers of stockings on each foot.

Bill Denny had a deep and gruff voice. At one time the small drill steel coming into the mine would not hold up. This particular steel drill rod had a sharper and greater twist than the other type generally used in drilling the softer ore. Any miner who ever drilled in hard ore knows the problems caused whenever the drill broke inside of the hole. This is especially true in the critical cut holes, hitch holes and back holes. With the defective steel, the miners raised supreme hell with anyone and everyone, regardless of how remotely connected with the steel, the man in the warehouse along with the blacksmiths who cut the long rods into desired lengths before pounding out the shank and bit. From the superintendent down to the captain and second captain, all got their share of hell from the miners. However the frequency and amount of hell was heard by the boss who had to go into the mining contract twice a day.

Bill had heard these complaints to the point of great frustration. One morning just as he was about to go into the mine after getting off the cage, the phone rang from surface. Bill was told to remain out shaft and wait for a factory representative from the drill company to come underground. (The heat over the bad steel finally resulted in the mining company insisting on a factory representative to come and look into the matter.) As Bill patiently waited, his anger grew. As the cage finally came down with the factory man, he was ready to take out all of his frustration and wrath on this man.

According to the cage rider, this looked like the first trip ever into a mine by the representative. A small man who wore glasses stepped out of the cage into the dim light of the mine. From the shadows he heard this deep and rough voice ask, "Is thee the son of a bitch from the factory?"

The startled man didn't know if he should jump back into the cage or not, but finally said, "Yes, I am."

Bill's only comment was, "Ye ought to be f_ _ked. Come along with me."

This did not relieve any fear that the agent had, but he quickly fell into step with the lanky foreman and followed him back into the working area. There he was greeted in the same manner by the miners who had waited a long time, like Bill, to meet any one who had anything to do with the problem steel.

Because of the slice method of mining, there were a number of mining contracts on the mining subs. As the ore was mined out on one sub, the miners dropped down approximately 13 feet in their raises and cut out a new sub. As mining advanced on each new sub, new travel roads connected the mining contracts. The same men worked for many years on the same subs which brought them closer to each other. Whatever and whenever help was needed they worked together, each man knowing what the other was doing. The first man I came in contact with after I was assigned a miner was a brother team of Art and Rudy Holapaa, a team of brothers-in-law Ed Peterson and Nels Anderson, Frank Numikoski and Gus

Peterson, another contract, Sam Carilli and Charley Rintala, along with another pair of contract miners John Ducoli and Angelo Zenti.

Wherever groups of men worked close together over a long period of time, the relationships between them grew stronger and continued out of the mine. This was especially evident in the mining subs where contract miners worked for many years on the same mining subs.

"Big Johns"

There were certain characteristics and movements that I remember of many men who I met and saw working underground. There were many "Big Johns" who stood out not only by their size but by their strength in lifting heavy timbers and moving machinery. John Olymaki was such a powerful man with almost brute strength. Watching him drilling with a jackhammer or breaking chunks with a chunk breaker made the work look easy. In his hands these tools looked like pistols and were handled with the same ease. John Kuivela, a husky Finn miner was one who never slowed down even in the hottest places. Never have I seen any man sweat like John, his overalls and shirts were always soaked with perspiration. John, like another hard worker, Rudy Johnson, could handle an ax as though it was a band leader's baton. Every one of the old experienced miners were masters in the use of their three to four pound axes. Axes used for framing timber and spraguing sets were special and maintained as sharp as possible. Let them catch anyone using this ax for cutting a steel rope or dulling the ax in any way brought immediate hell from the miner.

Before any cap was lifted into place, the miner would look at the top of each leg to see how much would have to be cut out of the joggles on the cap to fit the bevel on each leg. By sighting only with their eyes, the cap would be framed and when put into place fit as snug as if a bevel square had been used. These men did not hack the wood like a greenhorn but the cut would look like it had been planed instead of chopped with an ax.

113

"Big John" Ducoli, working in a neighboring contract, was about six feet tall and had a muscular body with strength and power to spare. This mustached Italian spoke English very well. Like others of his experience and age, he knew only work regardless of the conditions.

John and his partner Angelo Zenti came into a seam of extremely hard ore, which the miners referred to as "blue steel." Angelo, though shorter than John, was built with the same muscular body as his partner. I doubt if Angelo and John even really knew the extent of their lifting ability.

During a lunch period my father and I went into their contract to eat. Both men were holding up the jackhammer at the level of their foreheads. As we watched them pushing on the machine as hard as they possibly could, the drill didn't seem to move against the hard ore. The vibration from the drilling showed in the way the beams from their lights were bouncing against the breast. Soon they tired and their arms numbed by the vibrations. John stopped the jackhammer. He removed his hard hat and threw it down and said, "Dio bono, why you make this ore so god damn hard?" Not being able to understand Italian, I believe, in his frustration, he was referring to "Good God."

Angelo shook his head and said, "He crazy."

After lunch John's temper cooled. As we went back to our contracts, they went back to start drilling again. By some means, they completed their drilling and blasted as we quit for the day.

The motor crew liked to tease John. If they were loading the last train from John's chute, they filled each car to maximum capacity. The corner of the cars filled to the top and the ore piled so high that it reached the trolley wire. When John came down to the level, he would see how the cars were loaded. This would bring him to near tears. He would tell the motor crew that by this overloading, they were robbing him as well as the food from his family.

The motor crew kept a count of every car load of ore pulled from each contract by writing the number on a

114

chalkboard on the plat. The crew would tell the boss how many cars had been hauled from John's contract, giving proper credit for the number of cars that would have been loaded under normal loading. John, like other miners, had a fairly good idea as to how many cars came from each blast. The boss would have already credited John with the twenty cars or so that might have come from his chute during the pay period, but the tally would show only fifteen cars. This usually brought a loud protest from John and he would ask us or others on the sub to come and look at the tally and see how he was robbed once again. In time, John realized that he had received credit for the correct number of cars, since the average cars per shift for the pay period showed this.

As the end of the ore body on one sub neared, only the repairs that were absolutely necessary were made. At such a time the raise into John's place was severely crushed in. The men could not climb up the ladder road, nor could supplies be hoisted. The neighboring raise had to be used for these purposes.

Because of the small opening in the ore raise, the ore had to be scrapped directly into the ore cars. It could not be stored in the raise for fear of hanging up. John would bank up the ore close to the raise and wait for the motor crew to signal him when to dump the ore into the chute. Every time John felt that the car below was loaded, he would lean over the tugger and holler down to ask if the car was full. Again the motor crew would have fun by calling up to tell John, "Via little more." John would tap the handle on the tugger like a woman measuring flour into a cake batter. Little by little John would dump a shovel at a time down into the chute. The same procedure followed each shovel full. After a few more calls for a "little more," John would get mad and pull a full scrapper load into the chute saying, "Is that enough?" John didn't know that the crew usually anticipated this and had spotted an empty car ready for the ore.

Production

The Negaunee Mine set records for the production of a million tons for a few years during the war years of the 1940's. Conditions from mine to mine varied, and the miners at every mine were recognized for what they were – hard working, loyal and dedicated to their work. The difference between mine records was not in the people, but in the depth of the mine, type of ore, dry conditions, etc.

Of the three Cleveland Cliffs operated mines that were close to each other with the shafts running almost in a straight line, the northernmost shaft, the Maas Mine, and the Athens to the south were deeper and much wetter. The mine between them was the not as deep at about 1,490 feet. In time, all three became hotter in some areas due to the pressure and heat coming from the wood in the mined-out levels above. Some wood from the old workings was black and charred from the pressure and heat. The lack of air in the old mine areas, I believe, made it difficult for an actual fire to begin.

The Negaunee Mine employees were recognized for their production records. The men never forgot the cigars they received one year. The cigars had the name of the Republican candidate for county sheriff on them. They were obviously a campaign item left over from the previous election and transferred to a production award. I doubt if the candidate received one vote for every fifty cigars that were passed out to the miners.

Other prizes or awards that men often talked about were dinner pails that were given to the men at the Maas Mine. One man, Bill Perala, reportedly took his gift into the shop, put it under a press and flattened it. For this, he was called on the carpet. He defended his act by telling management that it was his, so he could do what he wanted with it. One year calendars were given to the men at the Negaunee Mine as they came into the office to pick up their due bills. Sippu Sivola was given a calendar, but before he got to the door, the clerk called him back and asked for it back. His father Vic had already got his calendar, and only one was allowed per family.

Chapter 6—Community Life

Food and Drink

The small Ann Street community of 31 houses had a number of families who owned two or three milk cows. The animals were housed in the two-story barns. Wooden stalls separated the cows, and winter hay was stored on the second floor. The cows supplied not only milk for my grandparents, but also for their daughters and families who lived only a few feet away—one family upstairs from my grandparents, one in the next house, and another across the avenue

As a youth, during the summer months I would go with grandma along the Athens Mine tracks and other areas where green grass and hay grew. With her sickle, she would cut the hay and tie it into bundles by twisting the longer hay into a rope and wrapping it around the center of the bundle. When we had enough bundles, a piece of clothesline was tied around them and we carried them to the barn. Even Atlas could never have been more proud carrying the heavens on his shoulders than I was walking alongside grandma carrying hay on my shoulders for my friends, the cows.

Since grazing areas were limited, the cows would be brought to wherever there was green grass. They would be tied to the end of a rope that was anchored to a fence post or stake driven in the ground. Leading the cows to graze and bringing them home had the same effect on me as carrying the hay.

For a long time I didn't know why grandpa took his cows to farms in Eagle Mills or the North Country. He would lead the cow two or three miles to the farm and return with the cow many hours later. About nine months after these trips, by some miracle a calf would be born. As I grew older I learned that the calf was not a result of a miracle, but a result of the cows trip nine months earlier.

Twice each day the milk bottles were washed with a specially made brush designed specially to fit the bottle. After scrubbing, the bottles were sterilized before being filled. All of the milk was strained through a clean cloth as it was poured into the bottles and capped.

As a young boy, I remember carrying milk to the Chetto family that also lived on the other side of the avenue, and a Nelson family below Maki's Hill. The one-quart glass bottles capped with a waxed cap were carried in homemade cloth carriers made from old bed sheets or pillowcases. The cost of a quart of milk was a nickel. Whenever there was any extra cream, it was used in a variety of ways. Poured into a large bowl or pan, the milk would be placed in a cool place. The cream would rise to the top and be skimmed off. This heavy cream could be shipped or churned into butter, used in baking, as coffee creamer, and similar ways. When bottled, the cream could also be carefully poured from the top and used by the family whenever it wanted whipped cream for strawberry shortcake, pie toppings, and homemade cakes.

The cream churned into butter also produced fresh buttermilk, and both were unequaled for taste. With warm homemade rye bread out of grandma's oven, they provided a meal worthy of kings. Grandma never used a pan for baking bread. She would start her dough the night before to make a sour starter. The next day she would add the necessary ingredients, carefully measured with her hand, and then knead the dough. When this was completed, the loaves would be then placed in the oven on brown paper bags or newspaper. Pieces of the newspaper often baked onto the bottom of the bread, but could easily be removed with the print still visible through the darkened paper.

In addition to my grandparents, I remember three other families with cows on our part of Ann Street: The Warmanens, Victor Rintamaki and Airaudis. Other families in Negaunee also had cows. At one time the city had a cow pound at the intersection of what is now Rail Street and Healy Avenue. On the northeast corner of the intersection, a lean-to shelter was built and surrounded with a high board fence and gate. Cattle running free were brought into the pound if the party finding the stray didn't know its owner. The pound was one of the first places checked by the family for a missing animal.

Not far beyond the pound, the Koski family on Maitland Avenue had a number of milk cows. During spring and summer, the Koski's brought their cows to graze in a large field on the south side of Ann Street and between Boyer Avenue and the Furnace Location. One summer morning, Mrs. Koski went to get her cows for milking. When she arrived at the grazing area she found only a big cave-in at the end of Boyer Avenue. What was once a part of a field was now a wide and deep hole. The surface had sunk into some of the old mined-out areas of the Athens Mine. As the ground disappeared, so did the trees and the Koski cows. I can't remember whether they lost four or six cows in that cave-in. For many days people came to see the sunken ground and hear the story of the lost cows.

Cows played an important and even critical role in the lives of many families. In addition to their milk and its many byproducts, cows provided much of the meat, and fertilizer for many gardens. There was a saying that one could not be sure if the cows paid for the miner's lunch, or if mining paid for the cow's hay and feed.

As a result of my experiences with grandma's cows, they became more like pets than mere cows. Families owning only a couple of cows had names for each. Though they kept no records of their breeding, they always knew which cow had visited which bull and avoided any inbreeding.

After a cow no longer could produce milk, it was destined to be butchered. This would take place at the beginning of cold weather in late November or early December. We knew the cow would be slaughtered when we saw the tripod and double blocks set up in the yard. Knives were sharpened and the meat saw made ready. A large crock, sometimes the butter churn, was placed near the tripod. The crock was packed in snow, ready for the blood of the cow. Special care was taken in bleeding the animal so that the blood could be directed into a small container and transferred into the nearby crock. To avoid coagulation, the blood had to be constantly stirred until cooled.

The cow was led from the barn to the tripod where it was either stunned with a heavy hammer or shot between the eyes. After the cow was killed and bled, the intestines and hide were removed as the carcass was pulled up on the tripod. The legs and head were severed and the carcass was left to hang and chill. It would later be cut in half, quartered and finally cut into smaller pieces. In the absence of refrigeration, my grandparents had a small shed where the meat would be put on shelves to freeze until needed. It was built out of rough lumber with openings big enough for air circulation, but too small for rats to get through.

The saved blood would be used in making blood pancakes and bread. These pancakes, which were almost black, were a favorite among many Finnish families, along with blood bread. French families used blood for making blood sausage, one of their popular foods. The liver, heart, kidneys, tongue, and cow heads were used in a variety of ways. Kidney stew might be made on the very day the cow was butchered.

The hide was sold to a dealer in hides, or saved for snowshoe lacing and other uses. The horns were often saved for stuffing potato sausage or for "kuppie sauna." By cutting off the point of the horn and hollowing it out, they made perfect tools for sausage stuffing. The kuppie sauna was a Finnish ritual and special event for many of the elderly Finns. One would have advance notice of this event. On our street, women mostly talked of it, and patiently waited for the woman who would come with her pail full of hollow cow horns and razor blades. As I understand, the patient, or perhaps victim is a better word, went into a real hot sauna. Small incisions deep enough to cause bleeding were made on various parts of the body, mostly on the upper arm, back of the neck and thighs. After the cuts were made and bleeding started, the horns were cupped over the cuts. The cupped horns drew blood like a vacuum, supposedly to clean or purify the blood and reduce blood pressure. It was easy to identify those who took part in this custom because they looked like they had fallen into a tank full of sea lampreys, with the round scars made by the horns and marks of the razor blade.

Though I had seen other cows butchered, it didn't seem to bother me. When I knew that one of grandma's cows—one of my pets—was going to die, it was a different story. Not wanting to show any emotion at the actual killing, I always found a way to stay indoors until I either heard the shot or felt that the cow had been stunned. Then I would find the strength to watch, but not enjoy, the rest of the procedure. To stir the blood was usually my job while grandpa, father, and a neighbor completed the job.

The Big Bull

Though many of the immigrant men were good at butchering cattle and other meat animals, the task did not always go as planned or expected. Many years after seeing the first cow butchered, I witnessed the killing of a big bull. Our neighbor Selim Jarvi came and asked my father if he could come and help butcher a big bull with a bad disposition at the Jarvi farm. Selim described the size of the bull and pointed out that it was just as mean as it was big. Selim's father Frank had this farm in the Eagle Mills Location. He kept a number of cows, and a bull for breeding purposes.

I was invited to tag along, and I did. Arriving at the farm, Frank and his wife took us into the barn. Seeing the bull, it was easy to understand that Selim did not exaggerate. Even though it wasn't disturbed, the animal's eyes were red and glaring. Both Frank and his wife were small in size, but it was decided that they would lead the bull out of the barn into another barn about sixty feet away. This barn was constructed out of long poles with spacing between each row of poles. Termed a pole barn, they were largely used to store hay and straw. A passage though the center of the building made it possible to drive into the barn and unload the hay. A three-foot-high partition wall ran on each side.

Plans were made and reviewed as to how the bull would be brought into the pole barn. Being familiar and knowing its temperament, Frank said he would lead the bull out of the barn with a long rope attached to the ring in the animal's nose. Predicting that the bull would rush Frank as soon as possible, another rope was tied to one of the front legs just above the hoof. The plan was for Mrs. Jarvi was to pull the second rope, causing the bull to trip and fall.

My father and I watched the ropes being tied to the animal. We decided not to interfere in the process and left the barn. Looking over that bull, we decided that the only prudent step was to climb up the steps to the house and hold the door open. In the event that the bull got loose, it would have to follow us to the second floor and possibly even a hasty exit out of an upstairs window.

Soon Frank came running full-speed out of the barn. His overall jacket was at right angles to his body as he ran out the barn door. Seeing the slack in his rope, it was easy to see that for every two steps Frank took, the bull took three! His wife didn't dare pull her rope and trip the bull inside the barn because injury could be brought on some of the cows.

As soon as the bull cleared the door she tugged on her rope, and the bull fell hard to the ground. The fall did nothing to the bull's disposition except to make it even madder. His eyes glared and foam shot out of its mouth and nose. It got up and continued to chase Frank. Before it got into the pole barn, he had to be tripped a couple more times.

While all this was going on, Selim watched and waited behind the wall in the pole barn. His job was to grab the rope from his father's hand as he ran through the door. Selim was to keep snubbing up the rope until the bull was securely tied to the wall. There it would be shot and butchered.

After his many falls, the bull was indeed a raging animal and kept bellowing and twisting to get loose. Frank didn't stop after giving his son the rope, but continued through the barn. As we watched from our vantage point, our bravery started to come back. Assured that Selim had done his job of securing the bull we went around the barn to where Frank left it, keeping our distance from the bull. I shall never forget the sight of Frank running out of the barn and his wife protecting him by tripping the bull.

A staple food, especially of the Scandinavians, was fish. Brook trout, lake trout, herring, pike, perch, and other local fish were eaten and cured in many ways. The traditional lutefisk available during Christmas and New Years was eagerly awaited every year. This dried fish came in big slabs that had to be soaked in water before cooking. Usually boiled and put into a white cream sauce, it was put over boiled potatoes. This dish, a heavy favorite of many Finns, was not one of mine. Anyone nearing a house where lutefisk was being prepared knows and will not soon forget the unique smell.

The families on Ann Street were, for a large part, self-sustaining. With their gardens, cows, apple trees, potato fields, and vast knowledge of storing and processing food, most people stored much of their food through the winter. In addition to the cows and pigs they butchered, wild rabbits, partridge, and deer brought a variety of meat to the table. A lot of their fish came from the Carp River, Teal Lake, Lake Superior, and Lake Independence in Big Bay.

During the fall, farmers from the North Country and Eagle Mills would go from house to house selling potatoes, rutabagas, and other garden crops. On a fairly regular schedule, those who raised chickens delivered fresh eggs and took orders for chickens that would be killed for holiday meals.

The only real needs not readily available had to come from the grocery stores, primarily coffee, sugar and flour. The per-capita consumption of coffee, based on a survey made by the Arco Coffee Company of Duluth, was reported to be the highest in the Upper Peninsula. I believe that the Scandinavians were the biggest consumers of coffee. According to state records of liquor sales, the people of the U.P. also consumed more brandy per person than anywhere else in the state.

Our Italian and French neighbors had expertise in making sausage, wine, moonshine, and many delicious native foods and breads. Some of the best salami was made by Italians in Negaunee. Their wines and moonshine were always in demand, and provided the makers additional income.

At the time I was born, Ann Street and its people had changed little from the day the first immigrants arrived. With its cheaply built company houses, outhouses and barns, manure piled no further than a few feet from the houses, the nearby active mines with their noise and dust, Ann Street would be considered by today's standards as low-income housing, or even a ghetto. I have always believed that the people within a community such as Ann Street make one's life more valuable and important than any house, whether it be a mansion in the best of location, or one like the place I lived in for so many years on my street —Ann Street.

An indication of how people were respected and remembered are the names given to certain landmarks. At the west end of Ann Street, there was a nice gray stucco house and well-kept lawn with a vegetable garden. On two sides of the lot was a green and manicured hedging. Occupying this house was a jovial Italian by the name of Joseph Spelgatti, with his wife and one son. Joe always had a heavy mustache and was very friendly, especially to the kids going by his house on the way to and from school or on our way to town. In the summer he would often have carrots and peas out of his garden ready and cleaned for us to eat. Even before my time this corner was called Black Joe's Corner in honor of this good man. Although both Joe and his wife have passed on, it is still called Black Joe's Corner by those who never saw or met him.

Two hills in the Ann Street area still carry the family names given to them many years ago. Midway on Ann Street, the smaller hill was named the Simon Maki Hill. The Makis lived near the bottom of the hill next to an open field where many families once raised potatoes.

My grandfather had such a garden next to the Maki home. Many hours were spent there during the growing season. (I don't believe that the mixture of Paris green and arsenic that he used to kill potato bugs would be available or permissible under today's environmental controls.) What had served as a potato field for so many families has been changed over to a trailer court. A new street runs through the middle of the old gardens.

The second and larger hill a short distance from Ann Street on the Queen Mine Road was named the Alongo Hill after the family that lived in the first house on the right a short distance from the top. Like Black Joe and Simon Maki, the Alongo family has passed away, but this hill will always carry the Alongo name.

There was a second open field between Queen Mine Road and the Karhi Road. The latter was named after the John Karhi family that lived on the south end of the field.

Those of my generation and earlier considered Ann Street beginning at Black Joe's Corner and continuing for about ten blocks east, ending at the Mattson family house. The last house south on Queen Mine Road was the southern boundary. An Italian that I only knew as "Chicken" Louie lived in that house, a house of great importance to those who enjoyed good moonshine. His advertisement appeared on the north wall of our barn. I know of no other wall that openly advertised illegal booze. Surely it was not necessary for the benefit of those living on Ann Street! They never had a problem finding moonshine. It was for strangers who didn't know where to go and what better place to advertise than on a big wall facing the street. The men who prepared the sign obviously didn't care about marring the wall. After all, it belonged to one of the mining companies.

Telephone

The only telephone in the neighborhood was the one in the hall of the Rintamaki home. It was never designated as a public phone, but it served the same

126

purpose. Whenever emergency messages involving any neighbor were received or sent, they came over this one telephone with the never forgotten number 127. Whatever the hour, day or night, one of the Rintamaki family would carry the emergency messages to their neighbors.

Wash Day and Chores

Monday seemed to be the day that most women washed clothes. Lacking running hot water, they heated water in large copper boilers. Before putting the empty boiler on the stove, the firebox had to be filled with wood and burning hard. Once the boiler was filled, it would be almost impossible to lift it to add wood to the fire. To fill it, cold water had to be carried in a pail from the sink.

Hot water was later dipped out and carried to the washing machine, usually placed near the stove. Though most families had an early model Maytag or other make of wringer washers, a few had only a scrub board. Absent of a wringer, the clothes would be taken from the rinse water and squeezed by hand. Some families had the old hand wringers that sat on a wooden stand. Clothes were wrung by turning the wringers with a side-mounted handle.

Washing machines were stored in a corner of the kitchen until washday. The strong odor of Bo-Beep ammonia and Fels Naptha soap filled the entire house and lasted for hours. The large bar of Fels Naptha was shaved with a knife into small chips then dropped into the hot water in the washing machine. Rinse water was in a large galvanized washtub set between two kitchen chairs facing each other to form a sturdy stand for the heavy water-filled tub. When the clothes were taken from the washing machine, they were run through the rubber wringers mounted on the washing machine. As the clothes came out of the wringer, they fell into the clean rinse water. After the first wringing into fresh water, the clothes were run through the wringer a second time and into a clothesbasket.

The last to be washed were the dirty mining clothes: woolen underwear, socks, shirts, and skullcaps. Overalls and jackets were never washed, but left at the mine and worn until they wore out.

During the washing cycle, it was inevitable that a lot of water would be spilled on to the kitchen linoleum. This made it necessary to mop up after the washer and tubs were drained and the washer shoved back into the corner.

The task of emptying the washer and tub was not an easy one. Water had to be dipped out of the tub and carried to the sink. Later models had a drain plug that could be opened. Dirty water ran into a pail to be emptied into the sink. Still later models had built-in pumps, and hoses that would pump the water directly into the sink. This made washday a little easier.

Every yard had clotheslines for hanging clothes to dry. Many had wire or hemp rope strung between the porch and barn. Others had two stands with clothes lines hung between them. Because of the ore dust from the mines and the soot from the coal-fired trains, clothes lines had to be wiped clean with a damp rag before any clothes were hung.

In case of strong winds, dust could blow from the mines and soil the wash before it was dry and brought inside. Should a stiff wind come from the south, it would bring dust from the Athens Mine; from the north, it would be Negaunee Mine dust. Failing to remove the clothes in time meant washing them a second time.

In the winter, the clothes would sometimes freeze before drying. They would be as stiff as boards. Inside, they were draped over the backs of chairs, over the tops of doors, on the heating oven, over the kitchen stove, or wherever possible. As the clothes warmed up and continued the drying process, the humidity would be so high that the inside of windows were covered with heavy condensation. Ultimately, they iced as the warm moisture contacted the cold glass. Moisture also clung to inside walls until the clothes were fully dried.

Self-Sufficiency

During all seasons, regardless of how hot the weather was, the kitchen stove had to have a hot fire to heat the wash water. The women tried to bake on wash day when the oven was hot. Soup would also be made to cook and simmer on the stove.

Men and women had little or no time for leisure or travel. Many never left the city limits after arriving in Negaunee. In addition to caring for cows, getting wood and preparing for winter, they also had many other things to do. Some bottled meat in vacuum-sealed mason jars, and canned wild blueberries, raspberries and strawberries. Garden vegetables were either stored in root cellars or packed in bottles. Jams and jellies were always made when the fruit was ripe.

What are considered hobbies now were necessities back then. The women made much of their own clothes and for their kids. Sweaters, scarves, mittens, tassel caps, and woolen stockings were knit out of wool yarn. Old clothes were cut into squares for patchwork quilts. Some clothing and old blankets were cut into strips for carpet rags which were woven with a hand and foot-operated carpet loom into long-wearing and beautiful carpets. Other women did beautiful work with their precision needlework.

Many men held other jobs in addition to working long ten and twelve-hour shifts at the mines. In addition to the cows and wood, they made their traveling skis. Skis, turned up on both ends and very narrow, were usually ten feet long. Ski poles were made to push through the snow. The bucksaw, sawbuck, and tripod used in butchering were among a man's most prized possessions. Even the large wood chopping block was considered valuable.

A good chopping block was not the easiest to find. It had to be big in diameter and one that would not easily split. To avoid rotting, the block was put in the barn for winter and kept there until it was needed. I know two boys who caught supreme hell from their fathers because of a chopping block. Kenny Cleven and I found a shoebox nearly full of roofing nails, or tarpaper nails as they were called then. We drove the nails into one end of his father's chopping block. By overlapping the heads of the nails, the entire top soon had a galvanized cover of inch-long nails. Surely Ken's father would be pleased with our work! The block would never rot or wear out and it would last forever. His dad had a totally different opinion. The splitting mall or ax would be dulled after hitting the nails. One lesson we learned was that it was much more difficult and took longer to remove the nails than it did to hammer them in.

A common sight in many yards was the large gray grindstone used to sharpen axes, sickles, knives, etc. These grinding wheels were at least two feet in diameter and near three inches in width. Mounted on a homemade stand, the wheel was turned with a handle at the end of a steel rod running through the center of the wheel. Old crank shafts made an excellent grindstone shaft with a ready-made handle. Under the bottom of the wheel, a piece of rubber tire or wooden trough was mounted to hold water. As the wheel was turned, it was kept wet as the wheel passed through the water. I spent many hours turning the grindstone as my father, grandfather and uncle sharpened their tools.

Snowshoes

Two of my neighbors, my uncle Jack Renfors and Pete Haikkinen, had a craft that was important to others. Uncle Jack made different styles and sizes of snowshoes. He would go into the woods to seek the special wood for the frames. I believe it had to be white ash with straight grain. This wood had to be split, planed, and sanded to exact dimensions to fit the forms used to shape the snowshoe. After soaking and steaming the sized wood, he bent and forced it into the form. Once anchored into the form, it would remain until the frame dried and the shoe retained its desired shape. Lacings for the snowshoes came from deer or cowhides. After removing all the hair from the hides, they had to be cut into strips approximately one-half inch wide and different lengths.

They had to be cut by hand, using sharp knives. The edges of the strips were scraped and rounded with a special knife. Leather strips were finally soaked in water to soften for lacing. The frame would be laced with the wet strips. As the strips dried, they shrank, making the lacing tight and strong enough to carry a person's weight. The final step in the process was to mount a toe strap and shoe binders, also made of leather, and finally to cover the snowshoes with many coats of oil and varnish to seal them from moisture.

Baskets

Pete Haikkinen, who was living upstairs of us, made beautiful wooden baskets. Three different sizes sold for one, two, and three dollars. Pete would go into the swamps seeking the special kinds of wood he needed. It had to be straight-grained green cedar. He sawed the cedar into four-foot lengths. After peeling the bark off, he carefully split it into one and one half inch widths less than one-eighth inch thickness. The light sapwood and the darker heart of the cedar made a checkerboard-looking basket. The edges of every strip had to be tapered by hand to remove slivers, then soaked for days in water to soften them, which made weaving possible. As he wove the baskets, the sides and bottom were interlocked, making an extremely solid basket. The top of the basket had a special weaving to maintain the shape and brace the basket. Looped handles were in the center of the basket. The final products were in large demand because people wanted them for a variety of uses. Many hours were spent watching these two men perform their craft with much-deserved pride and determination to make theirs the best snowshoes and baskets.

The Dreaded Steam Whistle

Living close to the two mines, we soon learned the meaning of the many sounds coming from them. Bell signals between the cage rider and hoisting engineer in the engine house identified the level that the cage should be raised or lowered. Similar signals between the skip tender underground, the landing crew at the shaft, and hoisting engineer controlled the operation of the skips raising the iron ore. The steam whistle signals between steam shovel operator and train engineer controlled the movement of railcars being loaded from the stockpile. Another steam whistle sounded at regular times: in the morning when men went underground, at noon, and at the end of the day shift. The most ominous whistle was the rapid short blasts that signaled the watchman to return to the dry immediately. This signal usually meant that some incident or accident had happened underground and the watchman was needed. Too often the signal meant that a worker underground had been seriously injured or worse—killed in an accident.

On a cold January night in 1937, the Negaunee Mine whistle sounded around 8:00 p.m. It kept blowing the rapid short blasts that ordered the watchman to get back to the dry. As the whistle sounded, we feared that something bad had happened at the mine. Little did we know what it meant to us. My mother and I were in the living room listening to the Major Bowes Amateur Hour over our small cathedral-type Crosley radio. Not long after, the kitchen door opened and my father rushed in. We knew immediately something had happened to grandpa, (Otto Marttinen) because they were partners and only my father came home.

He hurriedly assured us that grandpa was not dead, but had been seriously injured. Seeing the extent of the injury to his foot, the doctor sent my father to get Uncle Axel to come and take grandpa to the Ishpeming Hospital. The old ambulance was too rough riding and cold, and the doctor felt that to take him by ambulance would cause further harm to the foot.

We all went across the avenue where my mother and her two sisters stayed with grandma. I went along with my uncle and father to the mine to bring my grandfather to the hospital. As a boy of 11, I did not fully understand the extent of the injury, except that the doctor said that every bone below the ankle seemed to be broken and there were many compound fractures with some bones breaking through the skin. Fearing the very worst, I vainly tried to hold back tears as grandpa was carefully lifted into the back seat next to me. In the dim light from the dashboard and passing streetlights, I watched the pain in his eyes and on his face. He kept assuring me that everything would be all right, and told me to tell grandma not to worry.

Arriving at the hospital, orderlies were waiting with a wheelchair. I was not allowed to follow them into the hospital. I was told to wait in the car until my father and uncle came back. Sitting alone in the darkened car made it impossible to continue trying to hold back tears, and I sat crying and fearing the worst possible for grandpa.

Arriving back home, we went to see grandma to try and give her assurance that all would come out okay. Her eyes and expression left no doubt of her worry. Though the health of her husband of nearly fifty years was the most important concern, I'm sure she was also worried about their future, especially if he could no longer work. There would be no more paydays, no pension nor any source of income from his employer.

The extent of the foot injury was fully realized after he arrived at the hospital. There were no less than twenty-six fractures in the foot with the possibility of amputating above the ankle. For days he laid in bed waiting for a decision by the attending doctors. After ten days and demands of the family, it was agreed that he would be taken to the University of Michigan Hospital in Ann Arbor for examination that could possibly save the foot. Dr. Donald McIntyre drove grandpa to Ann Arbor, where the foot was saved with drastic surgery and bone graft. He returned home on crutches with a special built shoe. Later he was able to walk without crutches with the aid of a cane and with regular ankle high shoes. The Michigan Workmen's Compensation Law had taken effect shortly before the accident. A lump sum settlement of less than $2,000 made it possible for my grandparents to move to Alger County and take up a new way of life on the forty acres of land they owned. For his many years of mining, he ended his mining career with a payment of a few thousand dollars and a crippled foot.

The voices of the men working on the landing could easily be heard when the windows were open or when standing outside. Their words left no doubt as to what they thought about any difficulty they were having. As a kid, I could look out a window and watch the tram cars carrying the ore from the shaft to the stockpile. Sometimes the tram car door would get stuck or go off the track and one of the workers would walk along the trestle with a sledge hammer and bar and take care of the problem.

One of my memories is that even though our parents, grandparents and neighbors had more than enough work for any man or woman, they still found time for the kids. They would stop and talk and often tease. Seldom could we go into a house and not get a piece of cake, cookie or some other goodie.

Chapter 7 – War, Peace and the Mines

Drafted, Then Back To The Mines

Some time after I entered the mine and registered for the draft, the government stopped drafting the young men working in any of the defense industries. The iron mines were in this category and draft age workers were automatically deferred. This deferment did not last long and this policy ended.

In early June of 1944, I was inducted into the U.S. Army and sent to Camp Blanding, Florida, for seventeen weeks of training as an infantryman. Leaving Negaunee for Florida along with me were my classmates Wilfred Mallett and Bill Garceau. Other classmates were drafted from the mines or enlisted in the twelve months after graduation, then returned to the mines and worked for many years after being discharged from the military service. Among this group were Wilfred Bonds, Leonard and Gilbert Lukkonen, Stan Mager, Norman Heikkila, Nicky Lenten and Ken Anderson.

Wilfred was the son of Wilfred Sr., the mine captain at the Athens Mine. Junior was over six feet tall and had a strong body. Because of his size he had an obvious nickname which followed him even after the school years— "PeeWee."

After our military training we both came home on a two-week furlough before being sent to Italy. While housed in a replacement depot near Naples we were split up. My military papers indicated that my occupation was a "shaft sinker." This identification apparently covered all jobs in the mining industry as I never worked as a shaft sinker. Apparently because of some experience in handling dynamite I, along with a few others, found that we had "volunteered" for a special training course in demolitions. Returning after the two-week training I discovered that PeeWee had been sent to the 10th Mountain Division. Subsequently, I was shipped to France where I joined the 101st Airborne Division.

While stationed in Italy, I met my classmate and next-door neighbor Leonard Lukkonen and another boy from Negaunee, Emil Ghiringhelli. In short order we were split up and assigned to different units.

During the war, PeeWee's father and my father met during noon hour at the Athens Mine. Wilfred Sr., like all mine captains, came to the surface to eat lunch. When he was not on the day shift, my father would go to the Athens Mine to talk about any letter either might have received from their sons.

To my knowledge all of my classmates returned to Negaunee after the war ended and were able to go back into their old jobs at the mines. I don't have any recollection of meeting PeeWee after the war. He went to work at the Mather Mine where both he and his mining partner were instantly killed in a dynamite blast after hitting a mis-hole. What didn't happen during war ironically happened while working in the mine only a short distance from where he had grown up.

These classmates have, during their mining careers, worked in many different jobs, including that of salaried foreman and office workers. All were at one time members of the union while in production and maintenance work. Norman Heikkila was elected and served as a local union officer.

Back Into The Negaunee Mine

When I returned for work in July, the 104-day strike of 1946 had been settled a month and a half earlier. I expected to see open hostility between the miners and management. This was not the case, except for a few isolated personality clashes rather than hostility caused by events during the strike. There was a greater, much greater, air of hostility between the strike supporters and the few who broke ranks and crossed the picket line. These ill feelings lasted for years and in some cases even continue today. Many scabs may have been forgiven, but their actions were never forgotten.

I returned back into the same mining contract, Contract 36, as my father's partner. Many of the older men, for a variety of reasons, no longer worked at the mine. The mining areas had changed; some mined out, others were being developed.

First Purchase—Willys Jeep

As a single man, no longer facing military service, I felt more confident and secure of my future. The wages gave me a dollar and half more a day than when I left. This increase, along with incentive earnings, would give me the opportunity to buy things that had been only a dream in the past. My first purchase was a 1946 Willys Jeep. This was a civilian model similar to those used during the war. My canvas-topped vehicle cost about $1,400. This particular Jeep was by any measure a lemon when it came to starting it. Many times a call had to be made to Hill's Garage where Joe Kratz worked as a mechanic and wrecker driver. Joe would come to the mine and pull the stubborn vehicle down the road and onto Lincoln Street until it started.

The light jeep acted like a surfboard as it weaved side to side behind the wrecker. As long as I owned that Jeep, the starter never improved. Whatever was replaced or repaired meant nothing and I believe that a kid walking by with an ice cream cone was enough to keep the motor from turning over and starting.

At the mine, the biggest miner was Arne Juvani. A tall and heavy man, he had a hat size of eight and one half. His hat was broken and the mine didn't have his size in the warehouse. A special order had to be made to get a replacement. While waiting for the new hat, Arne had to work on surface. Casper Ranta suggested that I order the same size miner's hat and bolt it over the Jeep in place of the canvas.

Second Purchase—House

My second big purchase was to buy an old two-story house that had been condemned because of caving ground. Like a lot of the older houses, this was built of premium quality white pine. The nails were the cut nails shaped like a wedge, with square sides. These were easily removed without damaging any of the boards or framing material.

This seven-room house reportedly was one of the most popular during the earlier years. It housed a group of whores and was run by a madam. The entertaining tales and stories of this house and its operator were many. I tore down this building between my work schedule. It was well known by most of the men in the mine that I was tearing down a whorehouse that some looked upon as a landmark.

One day Pete Larson and his partner, Heikki Harju, were repairing in the travelling road between our contract and the neighboring one. Something happened that caused me to swear while I was working near the two timbermen. Pete, the same Pete who walked out of the church after his confrontation with the minister, heard me and came to me. Putting his hand on my shoulder and looking over his round-rimmed glasses he complained about my cursing.

Pete, according to his friends, was a different man during his youth. He played an accordion and frequented the blind pigs where liquor was illegally sold, and on occasion visited the house I was tearing down.

I asked Pete if he knew that I was taking down the famous house. He gave the impression of the innocent and having no idea of what house I was talking about. I told Pete that a few days before I had been tearing wallpaper from one of the upstairs bedrooms, and on one wall under the paper I had discovered a written note. The note said that Pete had played his accordion as a guest at the house during a wild party, giving the date of the event. There was no such note, but it brought a puzzled look on Pete's face as he tried to remember such a party. Uncertain, he again looked at me and said, "My boy, it isn't what you did yesterday or even today, what you do tomorrow and thereafter that is important." The only defense I could think of was to tell him that after I learned to play the accordion, to drink in a blind pig, and visit whorehouses, I would follow his advice.

The salvaged lumber from the house was moved to our yard on Ann Street. From there it was moved to land I had purchased in Sands Township. I paid $200 for this forty acres that had a small log camp on it. "Mud" Airaudi, a neighbor and friend, used the stake body truck of the contractor he worked for to move the lumber, first to Ann Street, and later to the campsite. The same framing was used as it was removed from the salvaged house, except that the new camp was only built as a one floor structure. The interior of all rooms were lined with three-quarter-inch pine paneling.

Most of the furniture was purchased from Raul Guyette, a bachelor living on Boyer Avenue. Raul was selling all of his furniture before moving to a furnished rented apartment. Forty dollars paid for a complete solid oak dining room. He also offered me a homemade still for ten dollars that he had used in making moonshine. The copper wash boiler and the tubing were in excellent condition and shined like new. I will never know why I didn't try to find the ten he had asked for the still. In hindsight this would have been a very authentic souvenir from that time.

Beatrice and Marriage

Not long after completing the camp, I met the girl I was to marry in June of 1948, Beatrice Juntunen of Eben. We first moved to an upstairs three-room apartment on Oak Street in Negaunee. Ten months later the mining company began selling their houses on Ann Street. The people who had been renters for the longest time were given the first chance to buy the houses. My parents, rather than buying the two-family house they lived in, bought a smaller house a block away.

Neither Pete Heikkinen nor his son wanted to buy the house after my parents turned it down. This gave me the chance to buy the ten-room house for $3,000 and move back to where I had lived before my marriage.

Within three years after our marriage our daughter and son were born. How comfortable and content could one be! Here I was with a fairly new jeep, a camp, a wife, daughter and son at age 27, and with a permanent job in the mine where I always wanted to be. I had already been elected and was serving as a grievance and safety committeeman at the Negaunee Mine.

With complete confidence in the future and raising my family, I looked to a future of happiness and security. The bubble burst soon after and the dream came to an end. Production was severely cut at all of the mines to a four-day schedule for three weeks, and no work in the fourth week. This lasted throughout the recession of the 1950s, with the fourth week being called the "Honey-Do Week" because the wives would be asking their husbands, "Honey, will you do this during the week when no work is scheduled?"

With such a drastic cutback, the contract miners worked even harder and in more dangerous conditions to make up some of the lost wages resulting from working only twelve days a month. I know of no miner who didn't do his best to continue providing for his family, even if it meant the added sacrifice and pressure on his body.

As the recession continued, I was forced to sell the camp that meant so much to me. It sold for $750, a fraction of what it had cost me. This money kept the wolf away from the door. Thankfully the mortgage holder, the Negaunee Bank, was patient and saw my family and others through this trying time.

Decline of the Negaunee Mine

The Negaunee Mine ore body was rapidly being exhausted after many years of high production. As the ore diminished in size, so too did the number of men. Some miners such as Sam Carilli and "Maggie" Koski left to sink shaft at the Mather Mine. Others went to the other Cliff operations on the range.

The final drift that Contract 36 worked was one on the fourteenth level. Special sets of timbers were put over the main line to give enough height to build a slide to scrap the ore up into the cars. Running at right angles and at the same level as the main line, it was unlike any other slice mining we had done.

140

Finally the former mining areas began to give and squeeze in as the weight and pressures increased. No attempt was made to keep these areas open. When trains or supplies could not be brought in, all mining ceased. Some of the tools and machinery were salvaged and brought to the surface but a lot got left underground. During the final days, Safety Captain Rodgers came underground and told us that it was regrettable that another new and similar mine like the Negaunee Mine wasn't available to keep the entire workforce intact.

One man came into the dry one hot summer night for the midnight shift. As John Olymaki was putting on his mining clothes, he told us what a terrible life the miner leads. Sometimes during the day John listened to a local minister talking on a radio. Apparently the minister railed and wailed in a typical fire and brimstone sermon. His problem was with those who drank alcohol in any amount, with specific reference to the miners who drank and that they were on the highway to hell. This didn't set well with John. He said, "One would think that coming here in the middle of the night to work in the hell-hole I'm working in would be enough to not be threatened with damnation by someone talking on the radio."

After our last shift at this mine, my father and I reported for work on the next Monday at the Athens Mine, a distance of two blocks from our doorstep. Many of the men at this mine were no strangers, as they lived on Ann Street and nearby. The first difference between the Negaunee and Athens Mine was that the latter was twice the depth of the Negaunee. It was also much wetter and generally warmer.

Athens Mine

The miners at the Athens had the same humor and were hard workers. Here too, there were family connections in many mining contracts. Angelo "Dinky" Carilli and Dominic "Puga" Jacobetti worked in the rock drifts. Floyd Cleven and his brother-in-law Vic Laitinen were partners. John and Charlie Mackey, a brother team worked together for many years in raise mining. There were the Petro brothers and Wills brothers.

Most of the Gwinn area men traveled to work on Negrinelli's bus, others in car pools. Names that come to mind are the Bianchi brothers, Johnny May, Earl "Bricks" Foress, "Little" Mike, the Taccolinis, "Finn" Catto, Joe Macarrio, Bruno Filizetti, Boggo Filippi, Chippy Juidici, Marttonen, and Big Henry Niemi. Many had worked at the Princeton and Austin Mines prior to their closing.

One man stands out in my memory because he worked near us and had a locker next to ours. Big Henry Niemi was a man well over six feet and had a body of nothing but hard muscle. He had hands the size of a shovel. No mine glove would fit them without being cut along the back to get the glove over his fist and wrist. I believe at one time, he was a foreman at one of the mines in Gwinn. While mining, he had Toivo Wilson as a long-time partner. The mine captain would know when Henry wasn't happy with the incentive rate that was calculated for the last half. The day the list came out, Henry would just sit down when the captain came in, and even though he wouldn't speak, the message got through.

Years ago during a statewide election, the people of Michigan voted to overthrow a ban that restricted the sale of colored margarine in the state. Only plain margarine with a packet of yellow coloring was legal in Michigan. The dairy people were adamant and waged a fierce campaign to keep the uncolored oleo. This was to protect the butter from more competition if the colored substitute was allowed. At the same time, there was another proposal as to whether liquor could be sold on Sunday. As Big Henry was wiping himself after his shower, he told us, "I don't give a damn if oleo is red or green, I want to get a drink on Sunday." The voters passed both proposals and the women no longer needed to mix the white oleo with the coloring to make it look more like butter than lard. Henry also was given the opportunity to go to the tavern for a drink on Sunday.

The dairymen in their losing cause argued against the artificial margarine. The advocates of change reminded the farmers it was they who started the change from the natural to the artificial. Long before the issue of oleo, many dairymen turned to artificial insemination of their dairy cows. Switching from the natural act of breeding with a bull, they denied the poor cow its annual date and pleasure.

Mining

In a short while my father and I were again partners and went mining. The Athens was like the Negaunee Mine in that most of the ore was mined by the slice method. New and different types of steel sets were tried in the hopes that the drifts would hold up longer under the weight. Instead of traditional timbers, Barrell steel, yielding steel, German steel sets, and heavy eight-by-eight steel was used. Some of the new methods of mining tried were block caving, grizzly drifts, and for a very brief time, the big four foot auger that was brought in. This huge machine was supposed to bring out the ore onto a chain conveyor and into the cars. The theory was to eliminate any drilling, timbering or blasting by contract miners. Once set up, the big drill would auger its way into the ore body and bring out finely-ground ore.

Whatever the theory or design and projection of the manufacturer of that monster failed quickly and miserably at the Athens. Not long after it was set up and turning, the problem came. As the auger bored into the ground, it would stop suddenly when an ore chunk would get caught and wedge it so tight that the machine could not turn the drill. A small, thin repairman would have to go along the stuck drill with a chunk-breaker, making room for himself to get to the obstruction and free the auger. This is about all that Ernie Carlson did while the machine was being tested.

The mine superintendent at the time was T.A. Kauppila. Most would agree that his temper was on a short fuse, and when a problem persisted that fuse grew shorter. After he spent a half-day watching this machine grinding out but one car of ore, he came down the drift to where we were working. Every man in the mine already

143

knew how things were going with this expensive piece of equipment, but we still asked T.A. how it was working. He cursed the useless machine and the inventor, but more than anyone, the "god damn fool" who purchased it.

Not only was he wild over the machine, but it had been put into a prime area that was already developed for block mining, which was ruining it. According to T.A., the miners carried out more ore in their boots than the drill was producing. As he walked away, he said, "Four more days and if that f_ _king machine isn't working right, Ernie Carlson will take a torch to it and send it up for junk."

As he walked down the drift complaining about the auger, he came to a frieden where a fairly new three-man jumbo was parked. This big water drilling machine could not get into a normal sized rock drift, except for the wider areas around the switches. This, in his mind, was another foolish purchase that could be sent to the surface and left there.

Block cave mining was, as I understand, going to be a less expensive and faster way of mining. This method was used in some of the best ore bodies in the mine where ore could be expected to cave on its own, and the opening came large enough. A transfer drift was driven just over the top of the main level and across the body of ore which could be as long as a couple hundred feet.

At about sixteen foot intervals, single cribbed raises would be put up across each other on both sides of the transfer drift. These raises were eighteen feet high from the top of the transfer drift. After all raises were developed, a grizzly drift would be driven over the tops of the cribbed raises and the length of the transfer drift below. Timbers in the grizzly drifts had to be the largest available, more than 16 inches in diameter.

The legs were only seven feet long, two feet shorter than those used in slice mining. The caps were slightly more than half the length of the nine-foot caps used in other areas of the mine. These sets of huge timbers were put on top of hardwood sills that were flat on two sides and were ten inches thick and approximately sixteen inches wide. The legs were put on top of these long nine foot sills, with another square sill installed between the bottoms of the two legs on each set. These were about fourteen inches square. These spreaders were installed so that the top of the spreader was a few inches higher than the side sills. This provided a lip or stopper in front of the bottoms of the legs.

Once in place, the sets of timber rested on the nine-foot sills with the big spreader between the legs. This was an effort to keep the timbers from being pushed down into the ground, or pushed in by side pressure. The sets were put as close together as possible to get maximum support on the grizzly drift between the cribbed raises. These raises were referred to as finger raises.

In the grizzly drift, another kind of raise was developed. On top of the cribbed raise, two mill raises were put in. A pair of the big sills would be installed at right angles to the grizzly drift. One or two sets of large cribbing would be put on the sills, forming a collar. From each of these, a naked or dog raise was put up to a height of about twelve feet. After the dog raise was developed, a dog drift would be driven connecting the mill raises on both sides of the grizzly drift and across to the mill raises in the grizzly drift on the opposite side of the transfer drift.

After all the mill raises were connected, the entire ore body was honeycombed with the mill raises and dog drifts. The transfer drift and the single compartment cribbed raises were common types of work for all miners. The grizzly drift, though quite similar to other timbered drifts, required much more heavy work, including considerable hand shoveling. The dog raises and drifts were the same as those developed in hard ore stoops, except that in block caving both the naked raise and naked drifts had to be made as small as possible to eliminate the added danger of cave-in, which resulted in larger openings where ground support was not used.

Due to the smallness of these raises, only one miner could work in them and do the drilling and blasting.

This was also true in the dog drifts, except that in the larger drifts one miner would shovel the ore back to his partner who would shovel it down into the dog raise. Because these drifts were so small, in most cases less than four feet high and as narrow as three feet, miners worked on their knees or crouched up. The best description of this work was that "it was like a dog f_ _king a jug."

Once all of the development was done, the miners went into the dog drifts and drilled long holes into the back and sides. The confined space made it necessary to angle the holes and use varying lengths of drills to get holes the desired length of about ten feet. At the bottom of the finger raise just over the top of the cribbing, other long holes would be angled to all sides, forming a funnel after blasting. Four miners, two in each grizzly drift, would follow this procedure from the front of the grizzly drift all the way to the end.

As all four raises were drilled they would be charged and blasted. I would guess that an opening of at least forty feet across would come after each set of raises was blasted. In time, an opening of this width and the length of the grizzly drift would be made into the body of ore. This would start the ore to cave on its own. The design was to draw the ore out of the mill raises evenly. The caving ore above would come down and not get mixed too early with rock or low-grade ore that would eventually come into the block as the best ore was removed.

This uniform and equal running of ore from the mill raises didn't always work out when large chunks of ore came down or ore packed in the mills. Often mills were tapped to keep ore coming. Mill runners ran the mills and were responsible for baring down raises that were hung up. Often they would use five-by-five inch blocks of dynamite put on the end of long staffs to bring down the ore by concussion. If that failed, ore miners would be called in to drill and blast to get the ore to move. As the ore was being taken out and the opening above the grizzly drift increased, the drift began to crush and twist until the mill runners had to crouch low or work on their knees to keep running ore out. At the start of drawing dirt out of a new block, it was not unusual for more than one hundred cars to be hauled out every shift. Two and even three motor crews could be kept busy by ore transfer drift scrapping out of a block.

In the Athens, drifts were supported by steel sets that gave the drift the look of a long barrel. Here a new and different kind of drill machine was used. Somewhat like the mill raises in the grizzly drift, mill raises were put in along these barrel steel drifts at intervals and across each other. A short naked raise would be put in at each location. The long hole-drilling machine would then be brought in and mounted in the center of the drift. Using short sections of drill steel, holes as long as forty feet would be drilled over the top and down the sides of the drift.

After a ring or more of these holes were drilled, they would be charged with a special dynamite that was two inch in diameter and about three times the length of the eight inch dynamite used in other blasts. Miners had to use a special set of charging sticks to push the dynamite into the holes. Many hours sometimes spanning over two shifts were needed to fully charge all of the holes in some of the blasts. Everyone in the mine knew when a big blast happened, as it could be easily heard throughout the mine and the people on surface could feel the vibrations. The basic difference between block caving and the long hole method on the steel drifts was that in the latter the ore was usually scrapped out of that drift and not run down into a transfer drift.

Any mining by whatever method has its inherent problems and dangers. Whenever a caving method is used, it's a soft ore mine in an area where the ore easiest to produce with limited ground support and miners. The Athens was the mine where most of this type of mining was attempted.

In the development of the block caving areas, there was the possibility of an unwanted cave-in or where a raise could "get away" from the miners if the ground formed a dangerous chimney-like effect running up into a raise that had to be cribbed and blocked. This would require a lot of blocking and supporting planks to save the raise from total collapse. In these situations, especially on the last shift for the week, were of concern to the miners. If left standing until the start of the following week and not properly blocked, the area would become even more dangerous, if not impossible. In two-shift contracts, this meant that the last men working on Saturday afternoon shift were the first ones to work in the contract on Monday day shift. Miners went to the surface to load whatever lagging and planks they needed to better protect the place and themselves for the following shift 32 hours later.

It was under these conditions that the company posted a new safety rule. Effective April 1, all miners would be required to wear their safety glasses at all times—from the time they picked up their brass check at the beginning of the shift until they returned at the end of the shift. There would be no excuses for not wearing glasses, except for cleaning them. This also included lunch periods.

We were in the process of trying to block a cave-in or ore raise when "Cap" Tippet saw me without my glasses on and warned me of the new rule. I asked him to come into the raise and see if wearing the glasses didn't create an even greater hazard by reducing visibility. He agreed, and said no more.

Vaino's Tale

The next day when he came into our contract, he laughed and told of his confrontation with Vaino Himaka after leaving our place the day before. Vaino and his partner, Joe Bollero, were drilling in rock with a dry machine and both were wearing their dust respirators. Tippet then jumped them for not wearing their safety glasses and gave them a warning. Vaino, who had a round face and small nose, responded by telling the captain that they better start looking for women who would go to bed with horses. Himaka said that a woman having a baby boy from screwing a horse would create the

148

ideal miner, one who had a long face with room enough for both the goggles and the mossier (respirator).

Vaino had the ability to come up with a story faster than any other person I have known. He spoke with a strong Finnish accent, leading most to believe he had been born in Finland. This was not the case, as he was born on Finn Alley in Negaunee. At age four, he went to Finland where he lived until joining the merchant marine. This job took him to many countries, including Australia where he stayed for a brief time. One of his stories included working and sailing in the merchant marine. On one boat he said he had one mean son-of-a-bitch deck officer directing the men working on deck. Vaino said, "That dirty bugger always gave Vaino the dirtiest and hardest jobs."

At one point it got so bad that he decided to take enough food from the galley and hide in one of the lifeboats hung over the side of the ship. After three nights in hiding, a bad storm came and almost filled the lifeboat with water. Vaino had no other recourse but to get out of the flooded boat and back on deck. No sooner had he got on the deck than the hated officer came running, raising all kinds of hell and asking Vaino where he had been hiding so long. Vaino clenched his fist, shook it under the nose of the officer and told him to shut his bloody mouth and not accuse him of hiding anywhere. Vaino said, "I fell overboard three days ago and it took me this long to swim after you and catch up."

Vaino had a definition of the difference between lying and bullshit. One may believe or not believe anyone's lying but nobody ever believes anyone's bullshit.

One of the first areas we ate in at the Athens Mine was in the dead end of a main drift. This was a dry area with poor ventilation, but remained out of the smoke coming from the miner's blasting. On the timbers and blocking were big growths of fungus that looked a lot like toadstools. Small field mice were always present, scampering around discarded lunch papers and food scraps. We mentioned the countless rats that ran around the Negaunee Mine underground. Those who had never been in the Negaunee Mine or heard of these big ugly and mangy rats had some difficulty in believing this. For some unknown reason no rats were ever seen in the Athens Mine, even though there were small passageways between them in a few locations. On the other hand we had never seen a mouse at the Negaunee Mine.

"Hell, the rat problem at the Negaunee Mine was nothing compared to the rats at the Mary Charlotte Mine," said Vaino. His story of this mine had been made in his mind as we spoke. He never worked at the Mary Charlotte or any mine during the very early times when miners used candles for light and mules pulled the ore wagons underground.

Vaino said that the caretaker of the mules at the Mary Charlotte always gave the mules extra rations on the day before Christmas, since men would be scheduled for Christmas Day. Then the caretaker had to report back two hours earlier than the others on the day after the holiday.

On this particular day the caretaker came as scheduled. As he got off the cage underground, he could hear a faint noise like metal striking metal. With his first-class hangover from celebrating the holiday, he thought it was only his imagination. As he went back into the mine, the noise got louder. Now he began to wonder what in the hell was causing this clinking sound.

With the dim light from the candle on his hat, he continued walking deeper into the inner workings. Each step brought the sounds louder. As he came around a corner, Himaka said there was a bunch of rats playing horseshoes. They had already eaten the mules and were now playing to determine the winners. The prize was to let the winner eat the harnesses previously worn on the backs of the mules.

Card Playing

When smoke and gas prohibited working, the men would play one of their favorite card games, smear. The afternoon shift on Saturday was tournament "night." Losers had to keep the mills full and the ore moving. The bosses knew what the men were doing and called up into the raise to see if all was okay. The cards were not made of plastic as they are today, but of pasteboard. A deck of cards didn't take long to change its appearance. The moisture of the mine caused them to swell. Soon the deck was three times as thick as when it came out of the box. The players' hands soon covered the face of the card so that the only way the card could be identified was to wipe a corner with a damp piece of toilet paper to see what the card was.

There were two occasions of card playing that I never forgot. One was in the dead-end drift on the main line where miners often ate. This was not a big area. Two drifts ran into the dead-end, leaving about fifty feet where the smoke didn't enter. During one particular lunch time, Second Captain Pete Bogetto came out of the smoke where a game was underway. He quickly grabbed the deck of cards and put them in his pocket. Pete was well-liked by the men, but for a day or two he was given the silent treatment as a way of protesting his action. This got to Pete, and when he went into the contract where "Boggo" Phillips and Sanford Kokko worked, he offered to give them back their deck of cards. The men laughed and told Pete to keep the mangled deck as they already had a new one.

Wilfred Tippet, the mine captain, had an experience that he made reference to many times. The "Greyhound," as he was called, had been on the upper level with two officials of Jones and Laughlin that ran the Tracy Mine just south of the Athens. This group had gone to check on the boundary between the two mines. This was a usual thing where mines were adjacent to each other with a common boundary. They would check to see if there was any evidence of one taking ore away from the other's property. For those who have seen fences separating two farms, they might have seen where cows on both sides of the fence had their heads on the opposite sides of the fence. We have all heard the saying the grass is always greener on the other side of the fence.

151

Like cows, the mine managers would have their miners come up to the exact boundary with the drift or slice. The miners would then drill long holes into the neighbors' ore body and blast and pull as much ore as possible out of their trespassing. This happened on both sides of the boundary wherever it was possible and profitable. There was no way in hell that any owner could prove that the neighboring company took some of its ore because there would be no evidence of timber or such across the line. When the drift or slice was complete, it was blasted down, leaving no possibility of any further entry or checking.

On this particular day it was near noon, a time when mine captains and other managers are usually on the surface eating their lunch. Many contracts had blasted and the only place out of the smoke was at the first switch coming off the main line. There were about fifteen men in the area, some in the process of eating, others sitting on a pile of dry planks with a card game underway. Cap Tippet and the visitors had climbed down a 200-foot raise about one hundred feet from where the men were. As they came out of the raise, they were in the thick smoke that was moving toward the shaft.

Not one of the men saw the three coming through the heavy smoke until the Greyhound was right behind Skeggs Hahka, one of the four card players. Since they were concentrating on the cards they held, it was not until the Captain asked Skeggs, "Why don't you shoot the moon" that a real scramble ensued. Cards were gathered up and the horseplay that was taking place on the planks stopped. It was easy to see that the Captain wasn't the happiest man underground as he turned and left for the shaft with the two men.

I am sure that he didn't eat his lunch that day, because it wasn't long after that he was back on our level. He went to each of the contracts that afternoon and reminded everyone of what he had seen. The most troubling aspect of the affair, he said, was not the card game or other activity. While he was making the tour on the upper level, he was asked about his workers and how

152

he got along with them. Even as they came down the long raise, the last thing Tippett had told the visitors was what productive and hard-working men he had, that the relationship between workers and management was extremely good, with very few problems. He told us it wasn't bad enough to see big Skeggs and the other players, but there was Joe Benaglo, an old man, wrestling with someone on the pile of planks. Joe was the hourly paid track boss at the time. Instead of looking like the men he bragged about, they looked more like the Katzenjammer Kids.

Uro in the Mine

Exchanging some of our lunch was a common practice—sandwiches, fruit, homemade cake, homemade salami, venison or headcheese. The latter is a favorite among the older Finnish people. Whenever someone butchered a pig, the head was given to someone who would clean it and make the headcheese.

Removing all of the hair and bristles from a pig's head is not an easy task. Uro Seppanmaa was a man who always looked for a pig head when butchering was underway in the fall or early winter. He made the head cheese which became a part of his lunch for as long as it lasted. One day as they were eating, Uro offered his partner Russ Kulju one of his headcheese sandwiches. Uro left and went back into his contract to put up the light cords, turn off the air hose and get ready to scrap the ore after their blast. Eli Lahti was watching Russ as he was eating the sandwich. Seeing that Russ was having some difficulty with it, he asked if something was wrong. Russ answered by asking Eli if he had ever tried to swallow a toothbrush. Apparently Uro didn't get all of the hair and bristles off when he cleaned the pig's head.

Uro was another of the older generation that had a good sense of humor. He was a stocky man who always had a squint in his slightly closed eyes. He was always ready to poke fun at others in his high-pitched voice and happier if one poked fun at him. Nothing seemed to trouble Uro and he enjoyed working in the mine. Like the majority of miners, he carried a glass gallon jug of drinking water from surface every day. When he got underground one day, his opposite partner told him that he had forgotten to take the empty jackhammer oil can out to the shaft to be refilled. This didn't cause Uro any problem. He poured the water out of his jug and filled it with the heavy black. For the next eight hours, the oil was more important to Uro than any drinking water.

"The Greyhound"

Mine Captains, second captains and shift bosses mostly came out of the miners' group. They personally knew not only the men they supervised, but the work of a miner. It was because of this that the bonds and often life-long friendships existed between many from both groups.

Most had good relationships and mutual respect with those they supervised: men like Stan Sundeen, Henry Moulton, Wilfred Tippett, Harry Cattron, Jim Maino, Pete Bogetto, "Finn" Cadto, Bill Denny, Ed Anderson, Charlie Bessolo, Abel Laitinen, Gus Jokinen, Bill Hares, Bill Skewis, Jan Cleven, Carl Luoma, "Skinner" Garceau and so many others. In most cases they worked before and after union organization and came from the ranks.

One man who held many different positions in supervision was Wilfred Tippett, the "Greyhound." He was a tall man who apparently took care of his health and was always in good physical condition. He walked at a faster gait than anyone I can recall and climbed raises with the best. During his long career, it was said he had walked the equivalent of circling the earth at least once and probably more. In making his daily rounds, he must have walked the equivalent of five miles every shift and hundreds of feet up and down every type of raise at all heights, averaging approximately twenty-five miles a week or 1,250 miles a year.

The Greyhound was a strong supporter and fan of all sports involving Ishpeming High School. Sometimes this support lead to his being asked and razzed when

Ishpeming was defeated by its arch rival, the Negaunee Miners.

During a district basketball tournament, the Negaunee Miners upset the favored Hematites from Ishpeming. The day after the game, as he made his rounds underground, Cap Tippett got a lot of razzing from the Negaunee fans. After taking this for many hours, he came to surface hoping to avoid any more razzing. As he was returning his lamp to the lamp room, Bud Reichel, the "lampman," reminded him of the game the night before. Tippett knew he was now on the receiving end, just as he had been on the giving end so many times before. What gave him the biggest kick was when Uro Seppenmaa came to pick up his lamp. Uro looked at the Greyhound and asked, "Who win the ball game?" Uro had already heard about the game before he came to the dry.

The two most dreaded trips into mining contracts for the mine captain, second captain or boss had to be the day the "list" came out. On the first workday after the fifteenth of the month and the last day of the month, the mine captain and superintendent would calculate the incentive earnings for each contract for the previous half month. Miners referred to these calculations as nothing more than turning a roulette wheel or tossing darts at a scoreboard. In either case, the men often argued that their pay had been calculated in less than a reasonable and understandable method. As the men with the list came into the work area, the first question was, "What did we make last half?" If the figure was less than anticipated, the miners let their displeasure be known in many ways.

Vaino and the Greyhound

The Greyhound never forgot how Vaino Himaka got his message across when one list came with a figure much less than expected. After Vaino heard of his earning from the boss earlier in the day, Captain Tippett came into his place. Saying nothing to the Greyhound for a few minutes, the Captain asked Vaino how everything was going. Himaka gave him the look of a tired man who was not feeling too good. He told the Greyhound,

I don't feel so very good. I didn't get much sleep last night. Asked why, he continued, I dream I died and I climb the golden steps to the pearly gates which was closed. St. Peter when he saw me told a engel [angel] open the gate, here comes Vaino, he been a good boy. When I get into heaven St. Peter right away ask if Vaino is hungry. I told him I ate just before I left. St. Peter called a engel over and told him to show Vaino around heaven. As we walked through heaven I saw a very beautiful place, Vaino said. Diamonds, gold and silver were everywhere and it was the nicest place I ever seen. After walking around heaven for awhile, I tell the engel that Vaino has to go toilet. The engel took me to a long room that was covered all over with marble. Along the floor were many round holes just the size of a nail keg. The engel told me to go into any one of the holes. After dropping my pants and beginning to squat over the hole, I noticed people below. I stood up and told the engel that Vaino can't go here because there are people below. 'Never you mind, Vaino, they're nothing but mining company big shots and you took enough shit from them down below. Now it your turn to shit on them.'

Tippett shook his head and turned to leave. Then Vaino called him back. He said as he was waking up he heard noises from above. He got out of bed and went down into the kitchen. "I heat milk and eat a little bit and done everything to get back into bed and sleep to finish my dream," Vaino said. Here Vaino was high up in heaven. "How could it be possible that noises were coming from a higher place above me? I couldn't fall back to sleep, but I just now know what that noise was. It must've been from that Cousin Jack heaven, because you always higher than the Finlanders." Vaino's disappointment over pay carried over into the heavens and above, and covered all of the Cousin Jacks in the world.

Measuring Progress

When it came time to measure the raises and drifts to calculate the bimonthly earning, either the second captain or captain would take out their tape and see how many feet the raise or drift had advanced since the last measurement. One of the miners would take the end of the tape to where the supervisor indicated the last measure ended. The supervisor would take the tape to the end of the work place to determine the exact number of feet advanced and to be used in determining the hourly rate. As he was walking to the end of the workings, a miner could accidentally move his end of the tape back a few feet, gaining an extra foot or so in the overall measurement. Credit for an extra foot really didn't amount to much, when a few dollars were spread over many hours worked in the full pay period.

Another game of sorts involved "pipe spilling." This was a way to install some protection in areas where a cave-in was probable because of the nature of the ore or rock. Long ten foot, one inch steel pipes would be put in before the blast. Long holes would be drilled wherever the miner thought necessary. The pipes, when pushed into these holes, extended beyond the distance that would be blasted. To drill the long holes required a special staging and the use of different length drills. Any miner who has used a ten-foot drill in a jackhammer will verify how it whips around as it is pushed in or pulled out of the hole. A rate of one dollar was paid for each pipe that was put in.

There came a time when management decided to pay for less than the ten feet for each pipe. The distance between the outside of the cap and the solid breast was deducted. This automatically reduced each hole by at least a foot depending on the diameter of the cap. In addition, the distance to breast from the front of the timber could reduce it by another foot or more. The further away from the timber, the more difficult to start a hole, and often more dangerous to the miner. To compensate for this change and resulting loss of a dime for each pipe also resulted in a change by the miners. After many blasts, many pipes would be broken into shorter pieces. These would be put aside by the miners. The next time they put in pipes, only a short hole long enough to hold the end of a short pipe was installed between some of the full longer pipes. Once in, there was no possible way to accurately determine its real length without pulling the pipes out.

This game probably ended with no real winner. For every deduction of a foot or more by the company, it was compensated for by crediting eight or nine feet for a pipe no more than half that length. At a dime a foot, it made no real difference in the hourly rate of pay, as it was either the number of cars of ore produced, or the distance advanced over the entire pay period.

Baldy Wills

In the beginning of my transfer to the Athens Mine, I worked briefly with two men who everyone knew and enjoyed. Baldy Wills, a slightly built Cousin Jack, was a longtime skip tender with a twinkle in his eye. Prior to getting on the cage at the end of the shift, Baldy started telling my father about the war between England and Finland, a war that never was. Baldy said he recalled a time when an entire division of the Finnish Army was marching through a valley and shots rang out from the top of one of the hills. Pinned down by the shooting, the Finn General ordered a Colonel to lead a charge up the hill with his entire regiment of over 1,000 soldiers. As the Finns slowly advanced, the shooting became more intense, enough to stop the advance of the charging Finns. Hours passed. Finally a soldier came running down the hill and shouted to the general, "Hurry up and send up another regiment, there's two Cousin Jacks up there!"

Dan Mongiat

A second man who without question worked steadily in the most miserable and consistent conditions, Dan Mongiat, a husky Italian—worked for many years in the Athens Mine skip pit. This area at the very bottom of the shaft had nothing but water, mud and cold. Water was everywhere, coming down the skip road, out of the rock around the pit. Overloaded skips would drag ore into the pit where it immediately turned into heavy wet mud.

Dan's job was to scrap the spilled ore into a buggy and push the loaded buggy onto the cage where it would be brought to the level above and dumped another time into the pockets. A small water pump was always trying to pump water out of the pit into a discharge pipe.

Dan always wore a waterproof jacket and pants over his regular clothes, and regular steel-toed hip boots. The heavy oilers and boots were hot. Even if water didn't come from outside, the sweat came from inside, making him wet and uncomfortable. Dan never, to my knowledge, looked for another job to which he would have been entitled. Even in the wet skip pit, he could take out a bag of Bull Durham, roll his own cigarette, and light it in the blink of an eye. Even more remarkable was how he could keep it burning.

He was also an unusual man who knew no pain. When on one of his periodic benders, he entertained others by chewing eggshells or biting off pieces of beer glasses. One time he felt a little pain and noticed an infection in one of his arms above the elbow. This condition lingered so long that Dan finally went to the doctor. An x-ray showed a long darning needle embedded in the muscle. This needle had been forgotten in his woolen mine shirt after his wife had darned it. Dan obviously felt nothing when he put his shirt on and in the process drove the needle deep into the arm.

As the ground continued to subside over the worked-out areas of the mine, the original dry house began to deteriorate until a new and temporary dry had to be built. The new dry was built right next to the sidewalk along Ann Street adjacent to the mine office. It was not a comfortable building. In cold weather, the frost was thick on the ceiling and ice formed on the floor. In warmer weather, condensation dropped like rain and the floor was always wet. During the coldest periods, wet mining clothes froze on the miner's chains instead of drying. The fans and heaters did not perform anywhere near what was expected.

While using the new dry, the Negaunee Mine shaft was being deepened. New levels and drifts would connect with the levels at the Athens Mine. Once this development was complete, the old Negaunee Mine and Athens Mine ceased to exist, and they both formed the Bunker Hill Mining Company. Still later, the men from the Maas Mine transferred to the Bunker Hill Mine and men from the old Athens, Negaunee and Maas were in one dry.

On Thursday, January 27, 1959, I worked my last day as a miner at the Bunker Hill Mine and as an employee of the Cleveland Cliffs Iron Company. This ended my working directly with the men I had worked alongside since that eventful day on June 22, 1943.

Chapter 8—Looking Back

Those of us who have lived all or most of our lives in a mining community, know that the community makes its contribution and sacrifices. Negaunee once rested on a huge body of iron ore. No one really knows the exact number of mines that have dug ore within its boundaries. As the ore was brought up from underground, it left openings and honeycombed the ground below. In time, as the mined-out areas became larger, the surface began to sink into the ground leaving visible deep, wide cave-ins. Old mining structures were destroyed by the caving ground and others slowly disappeared into the cave-in. Family homes and business buildings have been torn down or moved to safer locations. The Immanuel Lutheran Church was perhaps the largest of the relocated buildings. It was moved from Park Street to the corner of U.S. 41 and Baldwin Avenue.

The small communities of Swede Town, Finn Alley and others have disappeared. Where they once stood is now behind high wire fences. Other areas have also been fenced off to protect the public. Negaunee's one main business street no longer continues through Cornish Town to connect with the county road. All but two blocks of Iron Street have been placed behind wire fencing. The old cemetery located between the Maas and Negaunee Mines was relocated to its present location.

Cave-Ins

A sudden and unexpected initial cave-in came at the end of Boyer Avenue on the western end of Ann Street. I don't believe that the mine owners ever expected such an unexpected cave-in any more than the people. No one could have predicted the extent of this rather small area growing as wide and as deep as it already has. After the Boyer Avenue cave-in, the old mined-out areas underground have silently and steadily claimed more and more of the surface above. It has taken all of Boyer Avenue, the Furnace Location, a large section of the Patch Location, parts of Buffalo Hill, railroad tracks, five

161

of the old homes on the western end, and some of those nearest to the mineshaft and office area.

As a result, Negaunee has lost much of its original territory, with a resulting loss in people in the business and professional communities. The loss of surface area and all of the related losses, including the moving of our dead, does not include the untimely death of at least three young boys.

A four-year-old boy, Dale LaFreniere, fell into an abandoned mine shaft just a few feet south of the west end of Iron Street. The little boy fell into the open shaft and drowned. Desperate attempts were made to recover his body by lowering portable water pumps in the hope of pumping out the water. For days on end, these pumps continuously removed water from the shaft. The water ran down Iron Street and the people hoped and prayed that Dale's body would be found. This proved futile and a professional deep-sea diver was brought in to go down into the shaft and find him. After many dangerous attempts, the diver found the little body caught on a nail or similar projection from a shaft timber. As I remember, the boy fell down about forty feet before getting caught. The diver said that had he gone beyond that point his body would never have been discovered. Never before had the diver gone into more dangerous and dark water. He was prepared to stop any further attempts if he had not found the boy when he had.

Not very long after the tragic loss of this little boy, two 11-year-old boys lost their lives while sliding down the bank of the cave-in between the Negaunee and Maas Mines. As they slid down on pieces of cardboard, a large overhanging snowdrift on the rim of the cave-in broke off, causing an avalanche that buried and killed both boys.

Callous Disregard
These accidents triggered a more concerted effort to get a meaningful and enforceable Mine Safety Law in Michigan. Though miners had always made attempts to improve safety in the mines, it now became a community

concern to do whatever possible to protect the public from the type of accidents that we had just experienced.

I was one of the six local union officers who traveled to Lansing to attend a legislative hearing on a proposed Mine Safety and Health Law for the State of Michigan. Armed with the numerous newspaper articles and pictures that covered the two accidents, we testified before the 13-member committee. During the course of the hearings, a representative of a mining company sat silently in a corner of the room. At the conclusion of the hearing, we left the capitol building and the industry official remained with the committee. We left with no illusions of getting the majority of the nine Republicans and four Democrats to report the bill out of committee. After returning home we not only learned of the committee decision but sometime later received a copy of a letter from a downstate manufacturer of doors. In a one-paragraph letter to the committee, this nationally known manufacturer stated its opposition. The letter read something like this, "We strongly oppose the proposed Mine Safety and Health Legislation as it is patronage."

Never before, or in the years since then, have I ever seen or heard such a callous disregard for worker or public safety. I have no doubt that the writer of that letter and the firm that appeared on the letterhead didn't have a clue as to the mining industry, its miners or the people in the community. Neither party knew their ass from their elbow but yet saw fit to get involved and joined with similar opponents, including the single representative of the mining interest and those politicians in the committee who killed the bill. All continue to be equally infamous and their actions will always deserve the contempt of all people of good will and conscience who seek a safer way to raise their children.

I do not believe that there was one man, woman or child old enough to know who didn't support better safety conditions in their home town, and all other mining communities. I include those local officials of mining companies, even the one who sat so quietly in the hearing room.

163

As to abandoned and unprotected mine openings, it is noted that now more than four decades later, this issue is still a controversy. Current mine operators and those who most recently operated mines, have taken precautions and compiled with regulations, such as capping shutdown mine shafts and installing approved fencing and warning signs around dangerous or potentially dangerous ground. Many of the old mining operators have been long gone from the iron ranges of Michigan. By our current crop of state legislators, it appears that they are most reluctant to get the State of Michigan involved in making known safety and health hazards from abandoned mines safe for its citizens and visitors to Michigan. Where the companies have fully complied with regulations and laws, these sites must be regularly checked to assure continued safety. We, in the public sector, must also share some responsibility in our own safety by not trespassing in posted areas or destroying/removing warning signs. We should report any tampering or damage to the authorities, mine inspectors, or to the company.

At the Athens Mine, the first building to be lost to cave-in was the miner's dry house with the boiler room in the basement. Small cracks began to appear in the concrete floors and walls. Soon they became greater in number and size, and water pipes began to leak. Seeing the inevitable total loss of the dry house, a temporary one was hurriedly built right next to the sidewalk.

At about the same time, shaft sinking began at the old Negaunee Mine to deepen the shaft to the same elevation as the active Athens Mine levels. Drifts were then driven to connect the deepened shaft with the mining areas at the Athens. That completed, miners from the Athens Mine moved to the newly named Bunker Hill, and the end came to the Athens.

Today, the old Athens mine sites look more like an area devastated by heavy shelling and bombing in war. All of the old beauty is covered by weeds and brush. The two lines of tall Lombardy poplars that stood like barriers between the office area and nearby houses have disappeared, just as six of the nearest houses have. Broken pieces of concrete and brick are almost invisible with the long grass and weeds covering them. High on top of Big Hill, the rubble and rusting machinery can be seen. The shaft house, both old and new dry houses, shops, and trestles are on their way down to the bottom of the caving ground. Even the elevated railroad bed and concrete tunnel leading back into the mine feel the age. The tunnel is twisting and turning like a boxer hanging on, and the railroad bed is turned on its side waiting its turn to go under.

The Negaunee Mine (Bunker Hill) was never as visible as the Athens because it was not on a thruway. Its only vehicle access was a road extending east from the end of Lincoln Street. The buildings and structures, just as the Athens, are out of sight. Whether they have begun their descent into this second large cave-in cannot be seen, as they lie far inside the fences.

The third big area is located on the western side of town. It has taken much, if not all, of Cornish Town, Swede Town, Finn Alley, the business district, and the old streets and avenues in that area of town. Already, new growth can be seen inside these fenced-in areas.

The new Negaunee High School has replaced Mather B shaft and its adjacent buildings on top of Teal Lake Bluff. One of the mine buildings was incorporated into the new school. The school teams have always been the Negaunee Miners and may it never change. This will keep the memory of all of the men and women who worked in the mines alive, even though the mines have gone. In my opinion, the school sets on hallowed ground.

Unlike the huge opening left by open pit mining, the vastness and total dimensions of the effects of underground mining will never be seen by man—contrary to surface mining where the public can see how the pit grows in size and depth, beginning from the moment the first dirt is removed. People are impressed and awed as they see how large the pits ultimately become. They will remain visible into infinity unless filled in by man or nature—unlikely events.

What It Took

From memories dating back more than fifty years and from working at the Negaunee Mine, I will try to describe the vast areas that were opened up by the miners and what it took in men and material. No more unscientific method or mathematic calculations than this has ever been attempted.

The ore deposit at the Negaunee Mine began approximately 600 feet below surface. It continued for another 800 feet. The width and breadth of this deposit was limited only by the boundary lines between the adjacent Athens and Maas with the Negaunee Mine.

The method used at the Negaunee Mine to extract the ore was by slice mining, a method also used at the Maas, Athens, Bunker Hill, and Tracy Mines. I believe that all of these mines, sunk almost in direct line, were worked in the same big deposit with varying depths and boundary limitations.

In 1944 the Negaunee Mine produced a record of one million tons of high-grade and direct shipping ore. One has to visualize a big wedding cake with about eight separate tiers. Each tier has at least seven layers of cake, every layer about thirteen feet thick. The height of this hypothetical cake is 800 feet. To better illustrate what each layer was like is to look at them as giant thirteen-foot thick spider webs. By the time the last ore was taken out of the mine, there were about fifty-six layers of these spider webs one laying over the other.

In miners' terms, these were "sub levels" or "mining subs." A number of mining contracts worked on each sub, each weaving their own spider web as mapped out by the mining engineers, surveyors and geologists. After all of the individual webs connected, the sub level was finished and the miners dropped down another thirteen feet and started the same process over. To reduce these estimates for better understanding, I have used a single unit, termed "round" by the miners. A round was a cycle of drilling, blasting, removing the blasted ore and installing a set of timbers.

Material used in a miner's round "under normal conditions" would require the following:

144 feet of drilling (24 holes x 6 feet)
125 sticks of 60% to 65% dynamite
192 feet of blasting fuse
24 detonators (blasting caps)
3 thick 9 foot hardwood timbers (maple, yellow birch, or beech)
20 poles approximately 10 feet long for spieling, gin pole, back poles, spragues, stage poles
100 pieces of cedar lagging for covering and blocking
65 – 6-inch spikes to secure spragues, etc.

Every blast in a round would produce these averages:
100 tons of ore (20 cars x 5 tons per car)
936 cu. foot opening 13x2x6 = equivalent to a room size about 10x2x8 foot ceiling

These calculations would vary under different conditions, e.g., hardness of ore, wet conditions, heavy pressure, rock runs, etc.
Extending single round to 1,000,000 ton production:

200,000 trips of the 5-ton capacity skips to
240,000 drill holes
10,000 rounds (100 tons x 10,000)
1,440,000 feet of drilling
·1,250,000 sticks of dynamite = to 312 tons (2 sticks per 16 = 4,000 per ton)
1,920,000 feet of fuse
240,000 blasting caps
30,000 pieces of 9 foot timbers
200,000 poles
1,000,000 pieces of lagging
650,000 six-inch spikes

Total area opened in 1,000,000 ton production:

9,360,000 cu feet = equivalent to size 11 of 585 houses with 2,000 square feet of living space with eight foot ceilings or a tunnel or hallway ten feet high, ten feet wide and 93,600 feet long—approximately seventeen and one half miles. Distance from the Negaunee Mine to five miles east of Marquette.

The practice at the Negaunee Mine was to "pole down" the bottoms of the drifts and slices after the ore was mined. This was a grate-like pattern of ten foot poles spaced about a foot apart and nailed down to cross pieces. This was referred to as "gob" or "matting." The purpose was to form a cushion for the timber sets that would be drilled and blasted down on the poles to form a cushion of blasted timber, broken poles and lagging. What was originally installed to protect the miners on one sub was destroyed to add protection as he went under it to mine more ore. Approximately fifteen ten-foot poles would be nailed down with forty-five or more eight-foot spikes. This would add another 150,000 poles and 450,000 spikes to the total materials listing for the one-million-ton record.

These are the best estimates for the mining of only one million tons of ore. There have been millions of tons of ore taken out of the mines that operated throughout Negaunee for over a century. This gives one an idea of what it took to produce the ore; the men and material needed to open up the ground in that dark strange world deep under my hometown and the shaft houses of the Negaunee, Athens, Bunker Hill, Tracy, Mary Charlotte, Mather B and Cambria Jackson Mines.

Not included are the hundreds and thousands of pieces of cribbing, miles of rail tracks, ties, spikes, millions of board feet of two and three-inch hardwood planking, three-inch fir stage planks, miles of trolley wire, electrical wire, pipes of all diameters, timbers used for props in heavy areas, and a long list of other materials. More openings in developing raises, main drifts, haulage drifts, activities going on in all of these areas concurrent with the production of ore, all adding to the totals already estimated.

Over a thirty-year period, the men would average two rounds or more during each work week. Under this example, the two men would have produced about 200 tons of iron ore per week, 10,000 tons per year, and 300,000 tons in their lifetime. Installed over 3,000 sets and 9,000 pieces of timber, drilled on the order of 60,000 holes totaling over fifty miles. The two miners would have handled over 150 tons of dynamite in charging the thousands of holes drilled. They would have timed and lit over 60,000 fuses.

For every set of timber they had to sprague, they would have pounded in about sixty six-inch spikes with a four pound ax—while in every conceivable position. During the thirty years they drove in the equivalent of one spike 220 miles long into hardwood timber.

This only gives a picture of the lifetime work of the thirty-year veterans of mining iron ore in the underground mines. Many with longer service would have higher records than those who worked under better than average conditions.

The conditions under which the miners worked cannot be duplicated on surface. Depending on the age, type of ore and mining, the men would work under either hot or cold conditions, in poor ventilation or in drafty areas, dry or wet conditions, in open areas or in areas so small that a man could hardly crawl through. How many miles did these miners walk underground to get in and out of their work areas? I believe that a fair and representative distance would average two miles for every day worked. This means that the miner would have walked ten miles for every five-day work week, or 520 miles in a year, and over 15,600 miles in a thirty year period. I believe that this is equivalent to walking underground more than half way around the world. How many miles would the average miner have climbed up and down ladders during his career cannot be estimated.

The permanent closing of the Mather B Mine—the last underground mine— brought down the final curtain on a production that began at the time ore was first discovered in Negaunee in September 1844. Mines large and small, open pit and underground, from the most primitive to the most modern, have taken untold millions upon millions of tons of the rich ore out of my home town. Just how many mines and owners are unknown figures to me, as is the total tonnage produced.

One company stands out among all mining companies in the history of Negaunee—the Cleveland Cliffs Iron Company. When it decided to end the Mather B operations, its long history in Negaunee also came to an end.

Early in 1995, the Tilden Mine operations reached a high benchmark in its production of iron ore pellets. The Tilden, managed by the Cleveland Cliffs Iron Company is owned in partnership with other companies. When the mine reached the one hundred million ton level, it announced this achievement to the public. Mine Superintendent Robert Berglund appeared on TV and was quoted in the newspapers as he announced this new record of production.

I shared with many others the appreciation he gave to all of the retired and active men and women who made it possible. His comments were more sincere and conveyed a personal note than in most similar cases. I felt that he was referring to all of those who worked in the mines since the start of mining by CCI.

There are many records that have been set by those in the past, often broken by the same people. If history is any indication, the same loyalty, determination and hard work will break this new record if given a fair chance. This will be another test of wills for everyone associated with the company. It will involve investors, managers, supervisors, salaried and hourly employees whether in office, production or maintenance work. Given this chance in an atmosphere of mutual reasoning and responsibility, there is no question that Mr. Berglund or someone like him will someday make a similar announcement as they did at the time of the Tilden's record performance.

After the closing of the Mather, one question has often been asked. Will the day ever come when iron ore production resumes in Negaunee? After my experience of convincing myself that the Mather B Mine would last over my lifetime and beyond, I would never make the same mistake in predicting anything. Hopefully, the mines will return to Negaunee and bring back the kind of happy days of glory and boom times that were a part of my life.

There probably is more ore still underneath Negaunee than what has been already mined. It will be there until conditions dictate that the ore will again meet the demands of consumers of ore and the competition it confronts.

Chapter 9 - Christmas Eve 1943

After spending my first seventeen Christmases on surface, I now would be in that other world far beneath the surface. I was to receive a priceless gift, not available in stores or catalogs. This gift took only a few minutes, not years, to learn.

This came near the end of the afternoon shift on December 24th and involved an old Finnish miner I had first met many years before going to work at the Negaunee Mine. I had not seen George Hepola since the days as a young boy, when I carried lunch pails to the mine for my father and grandfather. George and I got reacquainted in June of 1943, when I actually began working at the mine. He remembered me as that kid who, along with bringing the lunch pails, could speak and understand his native Finnish language. As long as I could remember, his miner's hat had had a large piece broken off from its brim caused by a falling chunk. George walked with a slight twist in his body and always seemed as though he had many days growth of whiskers. He was about the same age as my grandfather, and they had known each other and worked for many years at the Negaunee Mine. Often George would ask how grandpa was doing as they hadn't seen each other since grandpa's accident seven years earlier, following which he had moved to Chatham.

What happened, near the end of the afternoon shift on December 24, 1943, because of this old Finnish miner, best describes how strong the ties were between the underground miners. At the time I had been working at the mine for six months and was still awed and learning more every day about this new world I had entered. Each day also increased my affection for the old miners as it still does even though they are no longer with us. A few days earlier, the surface crew had sent down a small evergreen tree that was set up at the landing area near the shaft. This had been a custom at the mine for many years and was very similar to the practice of putting a tree on the last car of ore leaving a mine as it shut down. The

172

trees were not the pretty and well-shaped ones we have in homes and in our community. This tree was about five feet high with few sparsely spaced branches, similar to the Christmas tree seen in the Charlie Brown comic strip. Miners stood it in a nail keg. Trimming the tree was left to the men underground and consisted of short pieces of unburned fuse, banana skins, toilet tissue and scraps of paper from lunch wrappings. Even though it lacked the bright and colorful decorations and the beauty of a nicely shaped tree, it was nevertheless, our Christmas tree.

Being Christmas Eve, the bosses took the men out to the shaft earlier than usual. With no oncoming shift and the ore pockets empty, the men would get to surface and home a little earlier. Arriving out of the shaft, the miners stood or sat in small groups talking and joking as they waited their turn for the ride to surface. I was among a group sitting on the long bench along the dumping area. Suddenly, a strong and beautiful voice was heard singing on the other side of the rock pillar that separated the pocket area from the landing area. Immediately, all talking stopped and, like iron drawn to a magnet, everyone got up and silently walked in the direction of the singing. As I rounded the pillar, I saw who the singer was. It was none other than George Hepola standing only a few feet from the tree. He stood holding his empty lunch bucket with both hands and seemed to be looking through the tree to the side of the rock drift on the other side. George was unaware of the audience he had drawn and kept on singing. Except for his eyes and the tree, his ore-covered skin and clothes blended in with most of the surroundings. This time, his eyes did not sparkle, or gleam or portray humor, but had that same haunting and indescribable look I had seen so often as a young boy. He was a man deep in thought over something only he knew. The eyes of all of the old miners were fixed on George as he sang his favorite Christmas carol like no other. Their eyes and expressions were the same as their friends as they stood silently watching and listening, as though hypnotized.

I often wondered what these old miners' thoughts might have been for those few minutes. Could some have been thinking back to past Christmases, family, neighbors, and acquaintances they left behind in their native countries? Or maybe to the war in Europe where old friends and a new generation of family members they had never seen were facing each other in the battles going on in old neighborhoods and hometowns? What were their grandchildren going to say, when they discovered that Santa had not brought all of the gifts they had asked him to bring? What would they say about the home-knit woolen mittens, stockings, scarves, hat or sweater that grandma had knit for a present? How long it would take to pay their friendly merchants for the extra credit they had given for the added costs of a few special foods for the Christmas meal and the few gifts they had bought? As the miners watched and listened to their friend's singing, they knew that their first paycheck in the new year would be somewhere between five and seven dollars less, because of the holiday. Not only would they suffer a loss, so too would their regular dining companions, the rats. The rats would not see any scraps from miners' lunches until some 24 hours later on December 26th. Some miners would return on the day after Christmas and find that their appetites were not normal. The excessive eating and celebrating of Christmas eventually meant more food for the rats. In effect, the rats recouped their loss with interest, but the miners never did, as their second paycheck in the New Year would also be short by one shift, Christmas.

Any stranger that might have come upon the scene could easily have been misled into believing that everyone there spoke and understood the same language. Though George was singing in his native Finnish language, the entire audience knew the words of the song. Had he sung in any other language, Italian, French, Swede or whatever, the audience would have appeared the same. The song George was singing was "Silent Night," a song, perhaps the world's best known, that was the same in whatever language it was sung. Any stranger to

Negaunee and the mine, who may have been watching, could not tell an Italian from a Finn, a Swede from an Englishman, a Belgian from a Norwegian, a boss from a miner, a Catholic from a Protestant, a Baptist from a Methodist, an atheist from a believer, a Communist from a Democrat or Republican.

What this scene portrayed during those few minutes was not a once a year event. This was the way of the early miners, whether at home or at work, they were as one. Standing together in the face of whatever they confronted. It didn't matter whether they were in the darkness of the mine or bright sunlight above, this relationship was the same among the miners. Above ground it was shared with their families and other townspeople. Together and wherever they formed a human fabric, not unlike the beautiful patchwork quilts made by the women during those early years. Those fortunate to own such a quilt have a piece of history and a priceless heirloom. The men in the mine, like the pieces of the patchwork quilt, were of many shapes and sizes, of many national origins, customs and traditions, and they formed this patchwork of men, held together and bonded with the strong thread between them. Just as the patch work quilts made by the ladies, both had been twisted, wrung, tugged, pulled and stretched in many different directions. The bonds that held them together never tore or broke. Like the beautiful quilts, the old immigrant miners are a part of our proud history and heritage, and equally priceless.

Nothing brought the people closer together than a family tragedy. In Negaunee and the other mining communities there were few strangers. Wherever sorrow and grief struck, it was felt by all. While death from normal causes brings sorrow, the loss of life in war and in the mines brought even greater grief. Many of the older miners spoke of a custom the miners followed in the early days of mining. Whenever a miner got killed in a mine accident, the miners would not go back into the mine until after the funeral. In most cases this would be for three days, days that no ore came out of the mine. There were no funeral leaves, or similar programs, that compensated their lost time. They chose to pay their deep respect and feelings of loss for a fellow miner. I don't know when that custom ended, but that respect existed for many years. This was evident to those visiting the cemetery and seeing old miners going from gravesite to gravesite of old friends to once again pay their respects and to remember them.

One old Italian immigrant typifies the character of that old generation. I knew Louis Satori for many years as a neighbor on Ann Street. I never knew whether Louie was married, as he boarded at the home of Mr. & Mrs. Batista Cavello. The Cavellos and their son, Dominic, lived on the Queen Mine Road, which we always considered to be a part of Ann Street. Louie was a timber hoister at the Athens Mine and had the nickname "Timber Lou." While eating our lunches a day or two prior to Memorial Day in the early 1950s, Louie told us that he had to go to the "flower store" the next day to pay a forty-dollar bill. For years he had arranged to have flowers put on the graves of his old miner friends. Clarence Rickland, owner of the Negaunee Greenhouse, would go throughout the cemetery putting flowers on these graves before Memorial Day. Louie said that these miners had no relatives in this country to put flowers on their graves. Many were buried without relatives to mourn their passing. Louie Satori's personal and annual remembrance and respect of old friends was ecumenical. Himself a native Italian and devout Catholic, his friends were all the same, in death as they were in the mines. Louie and the Cavello family have all passed away. A few years ago I visited his gravesite and from his gravestone, I learned that Louie had served with the American Army during World War I. It was rewarding to see fresh flowers on his grave and to know that he has not been forgotten by the friends he left behind, surely a fitting tribute to such a kind and thoughtful man.

Louie was not alone in his compassion and remembrance of old friends. Despite their hard work and lives, the miners were soft hearted, their feelings real.

While one admires and respects the many differences in religious convictions and the individual's right to believe as he wants, there are questions that will never find answers and perhaps are best left so. One wonders if the immigrant families and miners in Negaunee would have chosen to be segregated in death, after living in harmony and integrated with others, or if those who made the decision to be segregated in death had lived in Negaunee and worked in the mines?

Shortly after watching and listening to George singing "Silent Night," we were brought up to surface. For the next twenty-four hours, only a few men would be at the mine—on surface, a watchman and a hoisting engineer, underground there would be a pump man and two men on fire patrol. These were the only jobs during the three shifts when all others were home. The miners, like all Americans, would not celebrate the Christmas of 1943 in the usual way. The country was still at war and any celebrating or following of family traditions would have to wait yet another year.

The war brought many shortages and strict rationing on many items. Those who had cars couldn't find tires to replace old worn out tires. Art Samuelson's tire shop was one of the busiest places during the war years. Art would do his best to add a few more miles to the old tires as long as there was room for another boot and vulcanizing. Rubber inner tubes, like the tires, couldn't be replaced with new ones and the only hope was to continue adding patches as long as possible. Gas was rationed at four gallons per family per week. This meant that even those who had good tires on their cars didn't travel far to visit family and friends on Christmas Day, or any other day. Food items like sugar, flour, butter and meat were rationed and even with rationing sometimes unavailable. One housewife asked the butcher at the grocery store if he had any fresh meat. The butcher told her that all he had was beef tongues and ox tails. The lady reportedly told him, "Let the buggers who ate the middle eat the ends."

177

The miners spent their day off on Christmas the best way they could. Some in church, others getting into the spirit of Christmas with spirits. As midnight arrived on the 26th of December, the miners were back at the mine doing what they knew best, producing iron ore. They knew that they would wait another three weeks before receiving their next paycheck. The one that normally would have been paid immediately after January 1st had been paid a couple days before Christmas. It was paid early to give the miners a "little more spending money for the holidays."

What the Negaunee Mine miners didn't know at the beginning of the New Year of 1944 was that at year's end they would have produced a record one million tons of iron ore, a record once thought impossible. For this achievement they would be rewarded. Their reward was a cigar, still wrapped in cellophane, bearing the name of the Republican candidate for county sheriff. The cigars, apparently left over from the November election, were put into this secondary use. The miners never knew who it was that decided that these cigars were a proper award for this high production record. In turn, whoever it was could not have given any award that would be remembered so long. Many Christmases have come and gone since that Christmas Eve in 1943. Over these years, TV, VCR, video tapes and high tech recording have come into our lives. Special holiday programs, produced by professionals with top stars, come into our homes. Entertainment we would otherwise never see. Our homes, cities, business communities and churches are brightly lit with multi-colored lights and decorations. Church choirs and world famous singers bring their talents into our Christmas while dressed in the finest colorful robes. As impressive and enjoyable as these modern programs are, none will ever compare to the one I saw as an eighteen-year-old miner deep underground. There were no bright colored lights there, only the beams from the miners' lamps and a few bulbs burning overhead. There were no pretty robes worn by anyone. The program that lasted only a few minutes was never planned, directed or acted.

It was real. Despite all the differences, the real meaning of Christmas came through as if it had been put up in neon lights. The song George sang, in that environment while surrounded by true friends, the immigrant miners. It was a real life picture of brotherhood and what "good-will to all men really means."

This feeling of good-will and peace faded from most other places as quickly as the trees and decorations were taken down, and Christmas lights were turned off, the special programs ended, and the songs of Christmas went silent. The ornaments packed in boxes and stored away for another year, when once again the words of "peace on earth and good will to all" will once again be heard for the few days of the Christmas season. This was not the way of the old generation of immigrant miners and families. Though George would not sing "Silent Night" again until the next year, and the miners' tree had come down, the true spirit and meaning of Christmas would continue as it had for many years, the good-will between them continued, every day of the year. This was the priceless gift I received during my first eighteen Christmases. It was not a real surprise, however as it only confirmed what I had learned at a very early age living among the people on Ann Street. The good will and brotherhood I learned there was the same wherever these good men and their families lived and it didn't matter which mine they worked in.

Chapter 10—Santa Wore Mining Boots

When we live in that wonderful world of childhood, when life is without worry or care, we are told the stories of Santa Claus and the Easter Bunny. The talk of the make believe rabbit was short lived at home and in the neighborhood. We knew that eggs didn't come from any rabbit, but only from two sources. The teamster brought them as he delivered groceries, or they were found under the chickens in the neighbor's chicken barn. As for the rabbits, they were one of the staple meats we saw on the table. Had the horns of a reindeer been the same as on the white tail deer, the Santa story would not have been real for much longer than that of the Easter Bunny.

In our neighborhood and throughout my hometown, the story of Santa was told in many languages. From the start of mining iron ore, this small mining town had many different nationalities. In 1950 the Cleveland Cliff Iron Company conducted a survey of the 348 men at the Mather B Mine. They discovered that there were fourteen different nationalities working there. The Finns, with 136, were the largest group, followed by the English (52), French (45), Italian (44), and the remaining ten were represented in single digits.

Five nationalities were represented on Ann Street. All fourteen different nationalities, and I believe others, were present in Negaunee, twenty-five years earlier during my childhood. With my maternal grandparents and mother, who migrated from Finland, it was only natural that I heard the story of Santa in their native language and in English. It really made no difference whatever the language, this story was the same, as it added to those few, far too few, magical and mystical years of our childhood. How could anyone of that innocent age of make believe ever doubt the story of Santa? It was told by mother and father, grandma and grandpa, the people I worshiped the most.

The story they told was the most impressive and was filled with more anticipation and excitement than any other we heard. I learned how Santa and Mrs. Claus lived at the North Pole, 2,000 miles north of our house on Ann Street. There in his workshop, with the help of many elves, he worked throughout the year making the toys for Christmas. On Christmas Eve, Santa, on a sleigh laden with toys would race through the sky with his sleigh pulled by eight reindeer. As quickly as he came down the chimney and put the toys under the tree, he would go back up the chimney to race around the world to make the kids' Christmas wishes come true. Just a quick stop to eat the special treats left for him made his long journey possible.

Just as the Santa story is remembered, there are others that were related to it. Shortly after Halloween to be cautioned to be on your best behavior and manners because "Santa is watching," was a subtle warning that failing would mean the possibility of a penalty. The penalty, that every wish wouldn't come true, was easy to understand. As Christmas drew nearer, these wishes were seldom put in letters to Santa and sent to the North Pole. In many homes paper for any letter writing was almost a luxury. The three cents required to send such letter was a real luxury. Most Christmas wishes were given verbally to parents, grandparents and other family members. By some miracle they always reached Santa Claus. Neighbors would begin asking two predictable questions, "What is Santa Claus going to bring?," and "Have you been good?"

As the long awaited day came closer and the excitement grew, there were times when the dreaded words, "Maybe Santa won't be able to bring everything you wanted this year." When this happened, the high hopes and anticipation could go only in one direction— down. This happened to many of my age. Just when I was entering this magical time, the Great Depression began in the late 1920s. During those difficult years for the miners, we kids discovered that regardless of how we heeded the warning and conducted ourselves in the best behavior and manners, that these were not to be the Christmases we had hoped for. Being told to be good, even in the better years, often raised questions and dismayed many kids. From a personal experience, as the only kid, I received more than other kids in larger families. With six cousins living across the avenue I never was six times better behaved than they were or any better than any one of them. The toys I received brought hard feelings and bitterness from many who received less. Fortunately young minds are incapable of long-lived resentment. Whatever the disappointment resulting from comparing toys, it quickly ended. This came after sharing each other's toys and it wasn't unusual that by the afternoon of Christmas Day the toys were put aside, and the cardboard boxes they had come in were used to slide down the sand cut on nearby hills.

Those who told me the fabled story of Santa Claus, I later learned, had never had a real Christmas during their childhood. Our parents never expected, or realized, toys and presents when they lived in that magical age. If there were any gifts under the tree they would be woolen mittens, scarves, socks, sweaters or knit caps made by their mothers or neighbors. These came as no surprise as they saw them made over the course of the year. Hand-me-down clothes were made to look like new with a package of Rit, a dye for clothes. Grandparents, in most cases, had even less during their childhood.

I have no recollection of just when I departed from that make-believe world and discovered who my real Santa was. He did not live thousands of miles from our house but much closer. I didn't have to wait until Christmas to see him or hear of Mrs. Santa Claus. I saw them every day. Santa's workshop was not 2,000 miles from Ann Street, but 200 feet from our front door and 1,400 feet underground. In his workshop it was always dark, not unlike the long winter nights at the North Pole. In that darkness deep below ground is where my Santa worked with his many elves—his opposite partners and all the men on his shift. It was there where the kind of Christmas we would have was determined. It was not a jolly old Saint Nick that came home every day from the mine saying ho-ho-ho. His eyes didn't twinkle like those of the legendary Santa. They were the eyes of a tired and weary man. If there was work at the mines, it was the paycheck he brought home that would mean the difference in whether Christmas would be what we all wanted, or less. Unlike the other Santa who wore bright red and white clothes, this one didn't. His work clothes were all of the same dirt—covered grey and the only white was the white of his eyes. Both Santas had a slight similarity as they both wore belts and boots. One as a trimming, the other to carry a battery for his miner's lamp. One's black boots were always shined, the others' only for the first brief moments underground, because my Santa wore mining boots.

During those early Christmases of my life, the food on the table, as other treats, also depended on the money brought home from the mine. When times were better, the teamster brought a pound box of Queen Ann chocolate-covered cherries, a few popcorn balls, a bag of mixed nuts still in the shell, large oranges, red delicious apples, and a full case of twenty four six-ounce bottles of Elson's pop, the most expensive item, costing 80 cents. During these Christmases the older Finnish people, along with most Scandinavians, enjoyed their traditional Christmas dinner. The main course was lutefisk followed with a dessert of lingonberries whipped with egg whites. Anyone familiar with lutefisk doesn't have to be told about it. In early times it came into the stores like slabs of wood and had to be put into water to soften it and remove the chemicals used in making the lutefisk. Some say it was cured in a solution containing lye. Whatever the process, the smell of the fish soaking was unforgettable and it only got worse as it was being boiled on the kitchen stove. Its odor, something like that of a skunk or rotting cabbage, traveled far beyond the kitchen into the neighborhood. Regardless of odor or the work in preparing the fish, it was the overwhelming favorite of my parents and grandparents. The boiled fish in a rich cream sauce was poured over boiled potatoes. Though they really enjoyed this dish, the next time I eat it will be my first. As for the lingonberries, they have always been a favorite of mine. For myself, the distance between me and the lutefisk was never too far.

In those not-so-good years, special treats for kids didn't come and the Christmas dinners were different. There were Christmas days that began with pancakes made from the blood of a recently slaughtered cow. The meat on the dinner table might be beef or pork from animals butchered in the neighborhood or nearby farms. Venison or rabbit might also be on the table. Potatoes, rutabaga, carrots, and other homegrown vegetables were always available. At grandma's, there was her sourdough rye bread, biscuits and cake; butter churned at home with the fresh buttermilk that came from the churning; the homemade cake covered with canned berries from summer and topped high with whipped cream. Turkey with all of the trimmings did not happen very often. These turkeys could only be compared to today's by the color of their feathers. The plump tender turkey in today's markets are a far cry from those early scrawny and tough turkeys. White turkeys were not seen in the stores until many years later. Now in retrospect and after eating many excellent Christmas dinners, my thoughts go back to those many years. How I wish I could eat one more of those early Christmas dinners at grandma's with the family. This will never happen, but it doesn't stop the yearning.

After growing out of that carefree world, I learned that whatever the disappointment, the disillusion and despair I might have felt over the Christmases that fell short of hope and expectations, were shared by others, namely the parents, grandparents and others who could not fulfill the wishes of the young. While the young minds soon forgot, their disappointment lasted much longer.

Almost a quarter century after those early Christmases, I was another Santa that wore mining boots. Now the miners were experiencing a serious cutback at the CCI mines. This was called a recession not a depression. By whatever title it was called, it's effect on the men in the mines was the same as that of the

Depression in the 1930's.   Men with long service of twenty years or more were among the laid off.   Some did not return to the mines for seven years.   Those who continued working worked only twelve days a month, which meant a drastic reduction in earnings.   Like our fathers, we now realized how they must have despaired. The kids' disappointment over not getting what they wanted was nothing like that of their parents for not being able to give them all of their Christmas wishes.

Whatever our childhood experiences with Christmas may have been, the story of Santa must be continued and told to the young.   To deny them this would be taking away some of that magic and mystery known best to them in that worry-free and carefree time in their lives.

Coming out of all of my personal Christmas experiences as a youth and thereafter, I received the one experience most valuable and long lasting.   It was a gift that couldn't be purchased anywhere for any amount of money.   Even if the fabled Santa were real, he could not make this gift in his workshop.   This gift came from those many immigrant families that were our neighbors, and from my parents and grandparents.   What was this life lasting gift that meant so much?   The gift is never to expect everything you want every time by just asking for it—but as you travel through life never give up hoping and working toward the goals you seek.

Christmas 1943 was the last I would spend with the miners and people of Negaunee until I returned from military service in 1946.   As the New Year arrived on January 1, 1944, the miners started, as they had ended 1943, doing what they knew best, mining iron ore.   This year the Negaunee Mine miners would end the year with a record one million ton production.   I would not be with them for all of 1944 as I was called to service in June. Twenty-two months later I was discharged and returned home and to the mines.   During the time overseas I traveled through the homelands of many of my immigrant neighbors, miners and townspeople.   During this travel, I saw events that were radically different than what I was accustomed to.

As this is a story of personal Christmas experiences, military training and experiences in combat have no importance. After every war, the sights of combat and killing and maiming of military personnel are reported regularly, as they are seen in movies and over television. While covering the horror of war or those in combat, very little is recorded about the other casualties suffered because of war.

After the troop ship _Monticello_ docked in Naples, Italy, ending a fourteen-day voyage out of Virginia, a truck convoy was waiting at the dock. The trucks took us to a large Army Replacement Depot some miles away. It was this trip in late November that brought me into a totally different world. Between my arrival in Italy in November and February of 1945, I again learned the meaning of Christmas as I had before from the immigrant families of Negaunee.

As the convoy of trucks went through Naples and two smaller towns on the way to the depot, there were other sights that made their impression on me. Along the way old men and women sat on stairways and chairs with the same haunting look I had seen in the eyes of the Italian immigrant miners after the start of World War II. Those along the street had a more bewildered look and seemed puzzled by what was happening to their sons, the family, town and country. They had the same worries as the Italian miners and families on the Marquette Iron Range. It wasn't only the old who watched the trucks go by, but the much younger who ran alongside the trucks telling the soldiers what candy bars, cigarettes and ladies' stockings could bring from older sisters, mothers and other women they knew. These young boys were nothing but little street urchins acting like pimps and really didn't understand what they were doing.

As the convoy got near the depot, we could see women and kids running after Army garbage trucks on the way to the dump. Most were carrying two containers to separate the army leftovers. One was for any scraps suitable for the family to eat; food that wasn't fit for the family was put into the second container to feed pigs, chickens and any other animals they had.

One age group of men was not to be seen along the way. These were the men of military age and were men that many on the trucks would meet some other day —"Not riding on a truck but in their gun sights."

In that relatively short distance between the dock in Naples and the depot, I witnessed events that were as foreign to me as the foreign land I had come to. The look on the faces of the old generation Italians, the young chasing trucks selling women, the women following and often fighting over Army garbage, have never been forgotten and hopefully such scenes and events will never happen anywhere in America or be repeated in Italy or any other country. In the span of a few hours between the dock and depot I saw a side of life that I had never seen in nineteen years.

Though it was not actually Christmas Eve or Day, these events had happened a few weeks earlier and they came at a time when every man and woman in military service had memories of their past Christmases and was wondering about next Christmas and whether or not they would be there to celebrate.

Christmas Day was a cold, damp and rainy day. With the exception of those on guard duty and other assignments, most men stayed inside the unheated tents surrounded by ankle deep mud, unlike the warmth of home surrounded by white snow. A few days after Christmas, there was another boat ride, this time from Naples to France followed by a longer truck ride to that region of France called Alsace-Lorraine, which was near the front lines. After the trucks stopped at their destination in a rural area we were given two options. One was to be sent to a regular infantry division, and the other was to volunteer for the 101st Airborne Division. As a man of 19 and single, I volunteered for the 101st and its 327th Glider Regiment. The fifty-dollar monthly increase in my army pay was too much to turn down. It increased my pay by almost doubling the seventy-six dollars I was receiving. Though I was now in a different country and closer to the war, many of the scenes in Italy were repeated. There were others I would encounter.

The first came during a period of R&R, rest and relaxation. After spending two weeks on the front lines, we were marched to a small town approximately five miles in the rear. This march began as it ended, in darkness to avoid detection. After arriving in this town near midnight, it was the platoon leaders who had the responsibility to find places for the men under them to stay. The best places were the houses the people lived in. Without a house, there would be no rest and less relaxation. The house that our squad would occupy was the home of an elderly couple. Many looked upon the people living in Alsace-Lorraine as either French or German, depending on who was occupying the region. Most spoke fluent French and German. When German forces were present, they were German; when Allied forces were there, they were French.

As we waited to get into the house, the old couple was evicted from the house. Their tears and voiced opposition were of no help to them. Due to the dusk-to-dawn curfew and blackout, they were escorted by the officers to the homes of family or friends that would be their temporary homes until we left. This couple reminded me of many of my neighbors and grandparents. They were all about the same age and lived in comparable homes. The houses differed in their construction, as these houses, the outbuildings and fence around the yard, were built of rock or similar material. The yard was too small to raise grain for their livestock, so nearby fields were used for that purpose. Small vegetable gardens were maintained to put food on their tables during the winter.

There were many similarities in this family's homestead to those on Ann Street and in other areas of Negaunee. On Ann Street, in addition to my grandparents, there were the Warmanens, Airaudis, Rintamakis, and the Koski family a block away from Ann Street.

It was only after the old couple had left, and we had removed our backpacks and put down our weapons, that we found out how lucky we were to be put into this house. The first two priorities after removing pack and weapons, was to begin a search for some other kind of food than the field rations we had eaten for many days. The other was to find wine or other homemade liquor, but not necessarily in that order. Within minutes, both food and liquor were found. In the cellar, small barrels of wine were found along with some other homemade liquor, bottled vegetables and fruit were stored on shelves, white potatoes, carrots and cabbage were stored in small bins. We were not interested in the four cows in the barn, but in the chickens in the coop attached to the house. Due to the blackout, only the light from cigarette lighters or matches could be used. As hens were lifted off their eggs, the loud squawking must have been heard far beyond the dim light from the lighters or cigarettes. Many chickens suffered more than taking them from their nests, as they would be killed, plucked and dressed as quickly as possible. Because of the blackout and cold outside, what better place to clean the chickens than in a warm house under better lighting with the windows covered. Faster than the chickens were cleaned and cooked, the men got drunk on their newly discovered booze. As this was happening, a record player was found with a number of the seventy-eight rpm records that could be played on the phonograph. There was a similarity in this player to the RCA Victor owned by my grandparents. A large horn-shaped speaker was on the player along with a hand crank to wind-up the phonograph after the playing of each record. It was nearing dawn when the first record was put on the turntable. Except for those in the kitchen, the others were talking loudly, as only drunks can, and were still consuming the liquor as if it were their first drink. The record hadn't made two turns on the turntable and the loud voices stopped as if a light switch was turned off. It was now over thirteen months after that Christmas Eve at the Negaunee Mine in 1943. I was reliving that event of my friend George Hepola singing and the effect it had on

189

all of his audience. This time "Silent Night" was being sung by a boys' choir, presumably the Vienna Boys Choir or a similar one. Just as the other ethnic miners couldn't understand George's words sung in his native Finnish language, we didn't understand whether the choir was singing in French or German, but we all recognized "Silent Night," just as the Negaunee Mine miners understood the song George was singing.

The drinking ended for that night and the eyes and expressions were the same as those at the mine. Silently we sat thinking of the next Christmas we might celebrate, or if we would survive to celebrate it. After many plays that record was removed and replaced with other familiar Christmas songs in languages strange to all of us, but understood. After only a few hours of rest and relaxation, we had discovered what we sought and had a meal comparable to any gourmet meal. The effects of the homemade liquors had the same effect as the bottles on the top shelves behind any bar. Also in that short time we had had a late Christmas, but one of the most memorable, as we listened to "Silent Night" and the words "peace on earth and good will to all," in a language we didn't know, but nevertheless understood the meaning. The old couple returned to their home twice a day, early morning and mid-afternoon to care for the cows. It wasn't hard for them to see how their flock of chickens was dwindling, or where they were being dressed. The feathers under the beds and chairs left no doubt as to what happened to their chickens. A visit into the cellar also showed them how those supplies were disappearing.

As we left and the old couple returned to their home, who could blame them if the word bastard in their language was on their minds—not because of the pants we wore or of our place in the Army command. We didn't know where we would go to fight but, in any event, the odds were that we would always have food, even if it was only field rations. In a few days we had drunk most of the couple's wine and had eaten a lot of their food and chickens, and the odds were high against them surviving the winter as they had planned, as they now had much less than before we arrived. The sound of the Christmas music was still fresh as we walked away from the house. Somehow the words of "peace on earth and good will to all" seemed to have a hollow ring to them.

Though the war would end within a few months, there would be new experiences added to my memories. The first involved a small boy no older than 12 or 13. While we were on patrol, he was found hiding under a pile of hay in a small barn. As the hay was being prodded with rifle barrels, this boy sprung up from where he was hiding. In his military uniform he looked like Sad Sack of the comic strip, as all of his clothes were at least six sizes too big. He was understandably scared and crying, as he was looking down the gun barrels of the men around him. Due to a language barrier, it took a few minutes before he pointed to a large white farmhouse in a field above the barn.

One member of the patrol took the young boy back to where our vehicles were parked and earlier prisoners were being held. The others started toward the house, hoping that they would not be seen by those inside. One rap on the door resulted in a loud scramble on the other side. The door wasn't locked and was quickly opened to see three German officers attempting to climb the stairs to the second floor. They only wore their army britches, underwear and stockings. The remainder of their uniforms and weapons were found upstairs along with dress swords, watches and personal goods. These officers never expected to be captured. While they sat in the warm house playing cards, they had this young boy standing guard and acting as their lookout in the cold barn. Though embarrassed by the sudden turn of events, and standing before us out of uniform, they remained arrogant and were apparently cursing the young boy who let it happen.

There wasn't enough room in our vehicles for all those captured that day. Of the four captured at the farm only one rode, the other three walked behind. Had we known where the boy lived he would have spent that night and all that followed at home with his parents, as every young boy should. What we saw that day was not the master race Hitler sought. One cannot believe there is any mastery as long as men like these commissioned officers would go to any extreme to protect and save themselves at whatever cost, even using the young boy.

During the final weeks of the war we were stationed in the town of Berchtesgaden and not far from Hitler's Eagle's Nest high on a mountain top in Bavaria. We learned that between the town and the dictator's retreat, there was a warehouse loaded with liquor and Hitler's private game preserve. It was the warehouse and its contents that were of immediate concern. Rumors of the amount of different liquors stored in the warehouse proved to be true. The warehouse was used for storing only the best for Hitler's guests and his elite guard. Our first trip was uneventful, and five-gallon water cans were filled directly out of barrels filled with wine and cognac. Many full cases of other liquor were carefully balanced on the load. It didn't take long before most men in D Company couldn't walk two steps in a straight line. Somehow regimental headquarters learned of this and orders were issued to put the warehouse under twenty-four hour guard, and no one was to be allowed into the warehouse without specific written orders from headquarters.

These orders didn't set well with the men who took their grievance to their lieutenant. Lieutenant Tanner had nothing to do with the orders or any personal interest as he was a non-drinker. The complaints of his men were persistent and growing louder, and after listening to them, Tanner took steps to end them by making another trip up to the warehouse. This was his first trip and he took me along with him. Arriving at the warehouse, we saw the guard in front of the door into the building and knew what his orders were. By saluting the lieutenant we knew the fellow was a new arrival from stateside. It had been a long time since anyone saluted our lieutenant, because of his wishes not to be saluted. The guard, true to his orders, refused to open the door and to allow anything out of the warehouse. Tanner just quietly told the guard that he had been sent by the top command to pick up a full load for a scheduled party for the commissioned officers on the following night. Tanner informed the guard that he wasn't given written permission but, if he returned empty handed, all hell would break loose and involve the guard. Quickly the guard gave the matter second thought, and the doors opened. Once again a full load was taken not to the Regimental Headquarters, but into town where the first load had been brought and consumed.

Company D men had a re-occurrence of being unable to walk a straight line. We never heard anything about this second trip to the warehouse. If we had, there would have been demotions, including the lieutenant, who might have peeled potatoes for the rest of his Army career.

My fourth trip up the mountain was not for liquor or venison. Seven of us were ordered to the top of the mountain. After being driven as far as possible, we were left to walk to the Eagle's Nest. At the higher elevation the snow prohibited vehicles from being driven to the top. Our assignment was to search for any of Hitler's private guards that might be in hiding and to return after four days. There was no sign of anyone and, during those few days, we had an opportunity to examine the luxury of this place, also referred to as Hitler's Tea House by some. It was reported that all of the art works and most of the valuable items had been removed by the Germans. The Free French troops were the first of the Allies to enter the place. Reportedly they took what they could carry, when they left. Somehow the previous takers overlooked a well-disguised silver closet built into a solid oak wall. We discovered this by accident, and we were rewarded by the eight solid silver trays well hidden in the silver closet. Each tray bore the initials A. H. with the Nazi emblem and the name and trademark of the silversmith. The eighth tray was an "extra" for the seven who found them. As a token of appreciation that tray went to the lieutenant.

During the first seven months overseas before the war ended, I had seen and experienced events I had never seen, or even thought of, during all of my nineteen years. Lacking the required points for returning to the States and discharge, I stayed in Germany until early December and then shipped to Southampton, England, to wait for my return back to the States and home. The anxiety only ended when we boarded the *Queen Mary* for our voyage to New York. The luxury liner *Queen Mary* had been turned into a troop ship. The crossing to America took only a fraction of the time that we had spent on the *Monticello* on the way to Italy. Before departing England I spent my second Christmas overseas, and the weather and climate were no better than that of the previous Christmas in Italy.

Before the *Queen Mary* docked in New York we were told that our marching days were not over. The 82nd Division was one of the many units that would march down Fifth Avenue in a Victory Parade. We briefly stayed in an Army base in the state of New York as preparations were made for the huge parade. All along the parade route throngs of people lined the street. As the service men passed by, many cheered with tears in their eyes, knowing that many of their sons, fathers, grandpas, daughters, mothers and sisters would never march again, or even return. The long parade was showered with ticker tape and confetti falling from the tall buildings on both sides of the avenue. Many in the parade, especially those eligible for discharge, did not enjoy the march down the streets of New York as much as the spectators did. After leaving England, the only marching they looked for was in the direction of their homes. My trip home came on April 23, 1946, and I ended my Army career where it began at Fort Sheridan, Illinois. This base served as an Induction Center and Separation Center for the Army.

The experiences of my youth during the Christmas season and the events associated with Christmas are lasting, and never to be forgotten, part of my life, conscience and conviction.

The memory of that Christmas Eve in 1943 when George Hepola sang "Silent Night" before the underground miners' tree with his fellow workers watching, the BB gun, the sights seen during World War II, along with memories of those few wonderful years when the North Pole Santa was a part and hope of every young boy and girl, and the discovery of the real Santa, the one wearing mining boots. While all of these and others came during the first twenty-one years of my life, another, even more important in some way, came twenty-four years later on Christmas Day in 1970. While all of the Christmas memories during my first Christmases had taught me the real values and purpose of living, this one was different as it related to dying.

It came during a visit and sitting with a man nearing death, due to cancer. The fellow was a widower who lived with his son and his family after his wife had died eight years earlier. No one knows just when the cancer began, as he was an uncomplaining man with a high threshold of handling pain. The malignancy had become apparent as he began to lose weight and the pain exceeded even his high level of handling pain. It was only then, in late 1969, that he sought medical attention. This led to major surgery, after it was learned that the cancer had invaded his stomach. The operation was done at the Ishpeming Hospital and, after the surgery, the prognosis was not good. The surgeon advised the family that he had only a year to live. For a while after the operation his life was more comfortable and gave hope that perhaps the doctor was wrong in his prognosis.

After a few months the cancer again began to take its toll with loss of weight and the pain even more severe than it had been. At that time his strength was such that he could no longer go up and down the steps to his bedroom upstairs. A hospital bed was set up in the glassed-in porch downstairs next to the bathroom. From there he could watch and wave to neighbors, and family members who passed by. By looking north he could see the old sites of the Maas, Negaunee and Bunker Hill mines; to the south the Athens mine, where he had worked at each of the mines for a total of more than 40 years as an underground miner. As the pain worsened, the doctor prescribed a strong pain killer to lessen, but never eliminate, the pain. On this Christmas morning, I sat in the porch near his bed when I was asked for something he had never asked anyone. Always one who "didn't want to bother anyone" he asked if I would go to the medicine cabinet and bring him another of the strong pain-killing drug. This request was an indication of what was happening within his body, as it was the second time he took the drug that morning. It was now nearing the end of the year since his surgery in January, and it looked as though the surgeon's prediction was right. Asked if the doctor shouldn't be called to make a home visit and give him some relief, his response was characteristic as he said, "Why bother Archie (referring to Dr. Archie Narotzky)? I know I'm dying and he has done all that he can." Dr. Narotzky was the family doctor who provided the post-operative care after the surgery by Dr. Tom Mudge. These words were like getting hit in the stomach, even though his death had been predicted. As I looked at him, his health had deteriorated, taking all of his strength from his body. As I looked at and listened to him, it was impossible not to show my emotions. After a few moments, he looked directly at me and said, "I'm not afraid of dying, I never hurt anyone. I'm tired and I want to go and rest next to ma." (It was common for husbands to refer to their wives as "ma.") These words only added to the emotion and anguish, after being told that he knew his death was imminent.

I asked when he began to believe that his time after the operation was limited. After a period of six months after the operation he knew that the cancer had resumed its attack on his body. So rapid was his weight loss that smaller sized clothes were required on a monthly basis. He had no regret over having the major surgery. Since the operation he had seen his only grandson go off to college in search of becoming a doctor. In July, his first great-grandson had been born and was the only one he would ever know.

Our conversation ended when the pain-killing drug began to take effect and brought sleep to his tired body. Before leaving I looked at him and his frail

196

condition. Knowing that his life would soon come to an end, it was not easy to see this as he was always a man with a work ethic seldom equaled, never exceeded. One of nine children, he had had an unhappy childhood because of an abusive father, had been a hard worker and heavy drinker. As a result of this abuse, he had made a vow to himself that should he ever become a father his kids would never be treated as he had been by his father.

This man and the one he called "ma" had been heavy drinkers, until they reached their late 40s when they both quit abusing themselves with alcohol. This was a joint decision made without help or assistance from anyone, or from any organization. From the moment of making that decision, neither drank ever again. This did not stop them from visiting their friends who owned or worked in taverns. The only difference was that they discovered it was just as easy to have a cup of coffee or soda pop, as it was to order a drink of alcohol.

In today's media, so-called professional journalists try to get the victim of alcohol or drug abuse to blame parents or even grandparents for their situation. Thus personal responsibility is avoided. This couple, as others of that generation, would never accept, least of all agree to such diagnosis. The blame was not some hand from a distant grave of someone they never knew, that was guilty of pouring alcohol in their mouths. The blame was theirs to take, just as it was their decision to quit.

Sixteen years after his last drink this man reminisced about his years of drinking. It cost him plenty, and he knew that others had benefited from his drinking. They had camps, better cars and houses than he had. Perhaps his best advice was to those who resorted to drinking because of a problem they faced. Such a problem will never be solved while drunk, and it will still be there when you sober up, and even then it will be more difficult than it was originally. Trying to solve it with a hangover will never be easy.

Approximately a month after Christmas, his condition worsened to the point where he had to return to the hospital. Too weak to walk any distance, he was carried to the car that would take him away from home for the last time. The end came around midnight on January 30, 1971. The last family member to see him alive was his only grandson. The grandson was told that his grandpa would die that night and, in one of the few times he ever requested help, that night he asked to be helped to the bathroom.

During their visit, the grandson heard what others had been told by this man about his philosophy of life and the personal work ethic he followed during his life. These were not complicated or designed by others. His grandson was told the following:

- The best and easiest way to complete a job is to do your best.
- To take shortcuts and unnecessary delays makes the job harder and longer to finish.
- Whatever you do in life, whether digging a ditch or doctoring always do the best possible job you can. It may not please others, perhaps no one, but doing your best will always make it easier to look at yourself in the mirror.
- A watch isn't necessary while working either for yourself or for others. Your body will tell you when it's time to quit the work for yourself. Those who you work for will let you know when it's time to stop working.

Two hours later, his life ended. On the following Monday his body was escorted to the cemetery by family members, friends along with the pallbearers. Because of the deep snow and extreme cold, graveside ceremonies were held in the cemetery vault. There he would remain until spring before he got to sleep and rest next to his wife of nearly forty years.

As I was returning home after the services, the thoughts and memories of this man and his "ma" ran through my mind. These thoughts brought mixed emotions, knowing that the extreme pain would no longer ravish his body and he would soon be at the side of his wife to rest and to sleep. Both rest and sleep had not been there for him during the late days of his life. Though realizing this, I felt a great sadness and loss. I had known this man and his wife for all of my life. Now with his passing, I had lost two of my best friends. I had worked with him as an underground miner for twelve years. For thirty-five years we were hunting companions and involved in many endeavors. His death came at the age of 68 on the 30th of January 1971. When the time came to lower him, for the last time, underground and into his final resting place, he was reunited with his wife. He would be among those other miners who, like him, were Santas who wore mining boots.

The loss of mothers and fathers leaves a big void in the lives of those left behind. It is a loss that is irreplaceable at any time or at any price. Just as impossible as it is to replace our parents, the memories, teachings and values we learned from them cannot be replaced. These priceless memories will never be replaced or forgotten as long as there remains breath in my life. Such is not the case with most of the Christmas gifts I received. While a believer in the fabled Santa, those gifts have been forgotten with the passing of time. Of all of the gifts that came later, they also have been mostly forgotten with one major exception, the BB gun. Even this may have been lost in the years that followed, except for watching those who used it on Christmas morning. Their excitement was like that of young boys— boys who never owned a BB gun of their own. The BB gun didn't last long, the memory continues.

Many years and Christmases have come and gone since my father died. With each passing Christmas, the events and people of those earlier Christmases only confirm that these gifts of learning are the most important and valuable. I cannot tell how many times my thoughts have gone back to the singing of "Silent Night" by George Hepola before his fellow workers and to the effect it had on that audience. Hearing the same song, sung in a language that was unfamiliar, even while drunk, had and will always have a sobering effect.

I saw the good and the bad side of man in the many ways we live. Also the dignity and lack of fear of one during the last days of his life. Hopefully there will be a Christmas in the future when the true spirit of Christmas becomes a reality. That the words, "Peace on earth, good will to all," the real meaning of the spirit of Christmas, will not be limited to Christmas, but will exist everyday for everyone for all of the days of our lives.

Epilogue

The old immigrant miners and their families meant so much to me. They came to start new lives on the Marquette Range with little more than the clothes on their backs. They brought their many different ethnic traditions, customs, crafts and native foods. They also brought their strong work ethic with them and it served them well throughout their lives.

One of their sayings was, "As the twig is bent, so grows the tree." When they arrived, they were surrounded with the vast timberlands of virgin trees, trees of many species with their roots deep in the ground. The trees had felt the ravishes of nature for many years but always stood tall, straight and strong. History shows us that these immigrants also felt the wrath of nature and of men. Yet they stood as tall, straight and strong as the virgin trees. Their roots also went deep in the ground when they went underground to mine the ore.

Though I spent much of my life near and in the shadows of these good people, I would never come even close to their stature. Even knowing that many others have also failed, is of no comfort to me. What is comforting is in knowing that some others have succeeded. How much better we all would be, if more, many more, had become similar "giant trees" as our forefathers. Though this twig never grew to be like the immigrants, no one could be more pleased and proud of being a twig among them.

Glossary

This glossary is not the work of a mining engineer or some professional. The definitions are those I learned from the miners themselves in the three mines in which I worked.

Blind Pig— a place where alcoholic beverages are sold illegally; also called a speakeasy.

Block Caving— the process of opening large areas of ore by undercutting the ore under its own weight; first used in the Athens Mine and later in the Mather Mine.

Breast—the working face.

Cage—similar to an elevator; used to transport men and material underground.

Company Account—the minimum daily rate paid a miner for non-productive work such as replacing timbers destroyed in a detonation.

Contract—number assigned to each mining crew.

Cribbed—a raise that is lined with cribbing; generally made from tamarack wood.

Crosbys—U-shaped bolts used to press wire ropes together.

Dirt Road—that portion of the **Two-Compartment Cribbed Raise** down which ore and rock were dumped into the transfer drift.

Dog Drift—a small tunnel-like opening. Because of its size, miners could not stand upright; like dogs on all four legs, the miners worked on their knees.

Dog Raise—similar to a dog drift in size, but a vertical opening.

Drift—a nearly horizontal mine passageway driven on or parallel to the course of a vein or rock stratum.

Dry House—structure where miners changed clothes; the wet clothes they wore underground were dried here.

Dry Ass—something dry to sit on.

Finger Raise—naked raise running into the ore block.

Frieden—a spur or sidetrack off the main line where mine cars and machinery could be parked.

Ginpole—a strong pole installed between the cap of the last set and the breast.

Grizzly Drift—a small drift that is heavily supported by large timbers, or later steel.

Head Frame—the top structure of the shaft house that supported the pulleys that turned the cable as it ran from the hoist to the ski or cage.

Jack Pot—an accidental spillage of ore; the unexpected caving and water coming in to the work area.

Ladder Road—see **Ladder Way**

Ladder Way—that portion of the raise with ladders used by the men to get to and from their work.

Lagging—cedar that has been split and smaller cedar cut in seven-foot lengths, used in all types of blocking.

Level—horizontal passage extending from the shaft to the interior of the mine, also called the mainline.

Manway—see **Ladder Way**.

Mainline—all material, ore and men had to travel along the mainline to get to and from the main shaft.

Mill or Mill Raise—a) usually two naked raises were located above the grizzly drift; the ore was worked by mill runners into a cribbed mill and dropped into the transfer drift to be loaded on cars below; b) a cribbed mill that carried ore from the two mills in the grizzly drift to the transfer drift.

Mill Runner—men who worked in the grizzly drift to keep ore running from the block above.

Mis-hole—a drill hole loaded with dynamite that failed to detonate.

Mossier—a dust respirator.

Muzzler—name given to the **Mossier** by a Finnish miner who compared it to the muzzle put on a dog.

Naked Raise—a vertical opening that required no cribbing.

Peerless—a brand name for chewing tobacco.

Plat—an area adjacent to the shaft on each level, where motor crews dumped the ore into pockets for loading of skips to take the ore to the surface.

Pockets—see **Plat**.

Raise—a vertical or inclined opening or passageway connecting one mine working area with another at a higher level.

Rock Run—when a drift was being driven, the result of hitting a vein of soft rock from which water poured; this had to be stopped so as not to contaminate the ore.

Round—the completion of the cycle of drilling, charging, blasting, removing and sending the blasted ore down the dirt road of the raise and then to install and complete a set of timbers. Miners who left the area in the same condition as they found it are said to "have completed a round" during their shift.

Rubber Oilers—two-piece suits made of heavy rubber; worn over the regular clothes of the miner in wet conditions.

Sand Cut—a V-shaped channel cut through a rock formation and a sand hill along the western end of Ann Street; original purpose was to run a set of railroad tracks.

Shaft—a vertical or inclined opening of uniform and limited cross section made for finding or mining ore; the opening went from the surface to the depths of the mine.

Shaft Collar—the space around the top of the shaft.

Skip—a vehicle used to hoist ore from underground.

Skip Pit—the bottom of the shaft and lowest work area in the mine; this area allowed the skip to run below the lowest pockets to load with ore.

Slice—the term used when branching away from the first drift; by slicing the miners were able to mine out the ore body they worked in.

Sprague—the brace or support installed between sets of timbers.

Sub—horizontal openings between levels.

Three-Man Jumbo—large drilling machine riding on railroad tracks with three separate drills, one for each man on the three man crew; it was only used to advance the main drift and development work in rock.

Timber Hoister—a member of the three man crew that brought the miners supplies to their work area from the level below.

Trammer Boss—man who directed all the motor crews in the mainline.

Transfer Drift—a drift where ore came from above through mills to be scraped and transferred into an ore car on the next level or **Mainline**.

Travel Road—any convenient passage in the working sub through which miners could travel to a secondary escape route or another contract to assist fellow miners; over a period of several months the weight of the ore and rock would press these travel roads from an area of 9'x10' to a passage you had to crawl through.

Two-Compartment Cribbed Raise—a raise usually measuring 5'x10' and divided into two parts; one part held the **Ladder Way** and timber side through which timber passed and the other portion called the **Dirt Road** down which ore and rock were dumped to the transfer drift.

Whore's Dream—another name for a **Jack Pot** or any cave-in that demanded a great deal of hand shoveling.

INDEX

Accidents: See: Mines; surface accidents and public safety, 162-165.
Alongo, Tip: 12
Amusements and sports of kids: 50-57; card playing in the mine, 150-151; fishing, 55; movies, 59-60; pinochle, 56-57; shacking cars, 51, skiing: 51-52, skiis: 28-29, sleigh and toboggan riding, 52; snowshoes, 130-131; softball, 52, 56-57; sports, 21; swimming hole, 52-53.
Ann Street: 2, 12, 13; description, 2-3, 118, 125-126.
Athens Mine: 8, 9, 143-148, 164-165.
Attorneys: Mike De Fant and Aaron Lowenstein, 16.
Autobiographies: xvii-ixxi.

Barn, pole: 122.
Baskets: 131.
Bathing and washing: 6-7; in the dry house, 9-10.
Berchtesgaden: 192-194.
"Big Johns": John Kuivela, John Olymaki, 113; John Ducoli, 114.
Blee, Jim: 6, 28-29.
Blood letting or kuppie sauna: 121.
Bread: baking, 119; bakeries, 14; Finn tradition, 7.
Businesses: auto dealers and garage owners: Curtis Donnethorne, Wilfred Hill, Paul Honkavaara, Art Samuelson, Abe Wolfe, 13; bakeries: Kompsi's, Torreano's, 14; bank: First National, 16; barbers: Duquette, Honka, Lehto, Remillard, 15, Langsford, 15; beauty shops, 15; beer distributors: Lee brothers, 22; candy stores: Milton Lindberg, 45, Oscar Kultalahti, 13; cleaners: Bannon, 15; drug stores: Arnett's, Cronin's, 13; electrical supplies: Fritz and Keith Wangberg, 14; families: Collins, Levine, Lowenstein, Nyland, Perala, Thomas, Wehmanen, 12; glove factory, 15-16; grocers: T.L. Collins, Dighera, Guzzy Holman, Lindberg, Selim Mattson, Fred and Paul Ollila, Porky Robare, Winter and Suess, 12, Dighera, 44; heating and plumbing: Tamblyn, 16, Thomas, Warner, 14; hotel: Breitung, 16;

in Negaunee, 11- 16; insurance: Negaunee Agency, Tamblyn, 20; newspaper: <u>Iron Herald</u>, 15; newstand and convenience store: Jimmy Miller, 15; Pellow Printing, 15; photography: Waino Maki, 15; restaurants: Main Drift (Laiho), Negaunee Cafe, Hillbilly Restaurant, 14; service stations: Lloyd Anderson, Percy Dotson, Ernie La Cosse, Walt Neely, Ted Smedman, Adolph Violetta, 13; taverns: 22-29, Guizzettis, Chris Johnson, Lafkas family, Gus Makela, "Cullie" Nassi, Vic Palomaki, Rose Paris, "Fat" Ruona, Vic Tamietti, 22-23; terrazzo work: Alex Guizzetti, 14; variety store, 16; Violetta's bowling alley and music store, 14.

Carello, Battista: 96.
Cattron, Richard: 104-106.
Chard, Lambert: 6
Champaign, Frank: 6
Chicago & North Western Railway: "400", 2.
Christmas in the mine, 172-175.
Churches and taverns, role of: 22.
Cleveland Cliffs Iron Company: land office, 16;
Clothing: homemade, 129; "Scotch" caps, 26;
Cod liver oil: 45.
Company housing: 3-7, 139.
Dairy products: 119-120.
Denny, Bill: 111-112.
Dentists: S.J. Bossolo, Henry Nankervis, Roland Sangregret, Joseph G. Thomas, Ernest Whale, 17.
Dighera store: 44.
Dogs: use of: 39-41; for hunting, 57-58.
Dry house: 9-10

Environment concerns: 54-55, 72, 106-107.
Etelmaki, Levi: xviii.
Ewen, Michigan: 30.
Explosives: preparation and fuse shack, 10;

Finland, 2
Folk tales: See: Stories and tales.

Food and drink: angel food cake, 63; beef processing: 120-121; blood pancakes and bread, 121; canning: 129; chickens, 40-41; Christmas, 183-184; coffee, 124; cows and dairy, 118-120; egg yolks in coffee, 63; head cheese: 153; lutefisk or lipeäkala, 124, 183; moonshine, 125, 126; rabbits, 40; rye bread, 7; at the sauna, 6-7; storage, 5.
Fraternal organizations: 21.

Grindstone: 130.

Hepola, George: 172-175.
Hokanen, Mikko and Senja: 12.
Hospitals: Ishpeming Hospital, Negaunee Dispensary, Twin City Hospital, 17-18.
Hunting: rabbits, 40; deer, 58-59.

Ice from Teal Lake: 43.
Italians: bakery, 14; food: 38-39, 125; Dan Mongiat, 159-60; moonshine, 125; rabbits and polenta, 40.

Jenkins, Thurston S.: xviii.
Jewell, Jimmy: 84.
Juntunen, BeatriceL 139-140.

Kauppila, T.A.: 143-144.
Knights of Columbus, 21.
Knights of Kaleva: 21
Kultalahti, Oscar: candy store and political activity, 13-14.

Larson, Pete: 138.
Laundry: 127-128.
Lenten, Lefty: 12.
Lumber workers: 25, 27-28.

MacCaullife, Julia and Nell: 48-49.
Maki, Art: 6.
Maki, Simon: 125-126.
Marquette Branch Prison: 56.

Marttinen, Otto and Ida: 79; accident and retirement: 132-134.

Mine: accidents, 92-95, 131-134; Athens Mine, 141-148; awards and prizes, 116; block cave mining, 144-148; bosses, 101-106, 107-111, 143-144, 151-153, 154-; card playing: 150-151; clothing, 67, 111; lunch, 98-99, 153; measuring progress, 157-158; pay day, 87 88; production statistics, 166-171; rats, 86-87; smoking underground, 106-107; visit to the: 8-10; walking through mine property, 42-43; underground conditions, 95-98; working in the Negaunee Mine, 68-73, 81-117; working in the Section 16 Mine, 74-75.

Miners: at the Athens Mine, 141; attitudes towards, 47-48, 141; appearance, 9; concerns of, 1; influences of, 2; population: xvii; self-sustaining, 124-125, 129-130; wages, 23.

Mining: history of, xv-xvi.

Morrissey, Elizabeth: xviii.

Movies: 59-60.

Mudge, Dr. William A.: attitude and practice, 17-20; attitude towards unionization, 20; a Christmas stop, 62-63.

Negaunee: 9, 11; cave-in land and associated problems, 161-165; description of the town, 43-44.

Negaunee Dispenary: description, 17-18,

Negaunee Mine: 9; Christmas in the mine, 172-175; decline in productivity, 140-141; production statistics, 166-171; property, 42-43; record production, 185.

Also see: Mine.

Osterbotten Hall, 21.

Outhouses: 4-5; 41.

Palomaki, Vic: tavern, 25.

Payment in kind: 19.

Peterson, Ed: 88-89.

Physicians: Burke, Gulickson, Donald R. McIntrye, 17; William A. Mudge, 17-20.

Professions: 16-21.
Prostitution: 138.
Pynnonen, Arne: 37.

Rabbits: as food, 40.
Rag rugs: 129.
Rationing in World War II: 177-
Red Dust: xviii.
Rintimaki family, 3.
Ronn, Eino: 195-199.
Ronn, Ernie: biography, xiv-xvi; camp, 139-140; concerns going underground, 1; confirmation class, 46-47; deer hunting memories, 58-59; develops the autobiography, xiv-xv; end career as miner, 160; family and community ties, 60-65; grandparents, 6-8; mining, 66-80, 81-117; life after the war, 136-138; marriage to Beatrice Juntunen, 139-140; recession of 1950s, 140; reflects on miners, 174-179; Ronn family in mining, 73-80; schooling, 42-50; swimming, 46; World War II, 135-136, 184-194.
Ronn, Eskel: 75-78.
Ronn, Otto and Maria: 74.

Satori, Louie: 176.
Sauna: 6
Savo area, 2; legend, 2;
School: anti-miner attitude of teacher, 47-48; discipline, 45; life at, 42-50; public, 16; St. Paul's Catholic, 16; teachers and others, 48-50.
Self-Sufficiency: 129-130.
Spelgatti, Joseph: 125.
Stories and tales: absenteeism and patriotism, 104-105; the BB gun, 61-63; Jim Blee, 28-29; candy dispenser, 65; deer and the wood pile, 59; Maruke Dellangelo, 38-39; John Ducoli, 114-115; English-Finnish war, 158-159; the kitten and the outhouse, 4; Hakkola and the dog, 39; Heikki Harju, 25, 104, 111; Huck and the 7 tons horses, 30; hunting dogs, 57-58; Jarvi's bull, 122-124; Juvani's hat, 137; "Maggie" Magnuson's glass eye, 38; Major and the outhouse, 41; Mikko's bill, 12-13; mining, 93-